The Healthy & Fun Choices Way

A Guide to Self-Discovery, Living Braver, and Finding Joy Every Day

Kirsten Klug

Copyright 2025 © Kirsten Klug
1 2 3 4 5 6 7 first edition 8 9 10 11

This book is copyrighted © 2025 by Healthy & Fun Choices™ Press, a subsidiary of ID Graphics, LLC.
13888 SE 126th Ave.
Clackamas, OR 97015

ISBN: 978-0-9798173-7-3

Book set in Times New Roman - Regular, Bold & Italic
Cover & Book Design: Kirsten Klug

Inquiries: Kirsten Klug 503-314-6701
Bulk ordering is possible for wellness programs and conferences. Available to speak at conferences and meetings worldwide.
www.healthyfunchoices.com | www.kirstenklug.com

Overview: Embark on a transformative journey of holistic well-being and personal growth. You will learn how to bring Healthy & Fun Choices™ philosophies, while exploring the art of living intentionally and embracing the flow of life. With practical insights and inspiring stories, discover how to infuse everyday moments with joy, cultivate resilience, and create a life that harmoniously blends purpose and play.

Dedication

For my parents and children,
whose love and laughter keep me grounded.

For my teachers and guides,
who showed me how to turn mistakes into magic.

And for all of us—
finding our way, one choice at a time.

***All the flowers of all the tomorrows,
are in the seeds of today.***
–Indian Proverb

Author's Note

I'm so glad you've found your way here.

This book was born from a lifetime of curiosity, creativity, and courage — and a journey that taught me how healing and joy are choices we get to make every day. It's been written through late nights, deep breaths, laughter, and more than a few moments of uncertainty.

I live with Wernicke's Aphasia, which means writing, reading, and even speaking can sometimes feel like solving a puzzle in motion. Every word in this book has been typed, retyped, and pieced together with patience, humor, and heart. I also had to lean into AI technology to help me make sure what I was creating was truly beautiful for you.

But that's what makes this project so special. It's living proof that our voices matter — even when they come through differently. My hope is that Healthy & Fun Choices® reminds you that your story matters too.

You don't have to be perfect to begin. You just have to show up — curious, kind, and willing to keep going.

Welcome to the journey.

Let's explore what's possible, together.

— Kirsten Klug

Foreword

This book has been a journey—years in the making. Not because the ideas weren't ready, but because life asked me to live inside them first. I had to test what I teach, redefine what I believed, and learn how to listen to the quiet truths underneath all the noise.

Growing up, I thought life followed a pattern: work hard, love deeply, show up fully, and things would fall into place. But life moved in its own rhythms—beautiful one moment, bewildering the next. Success and struggle lived side by side. Joy and exhaustion took turns. And I learned, again and again, that being human is far from linear.

My children invited me to see the world through wonder—curiosity, giggles, sticky fingers, wild imagination, and the freedom to let things be messy. They reminded me that perfection is not the point. Presence is. And that every choice we make, even the smallest one, has the power to shift our entire day.

That realization grew into Healthy & Fun Choices®—a way of living that includes speaking up even when it's hard, finding courage even when in pain, and trusting that our imperfections are magical. I've lived through my own seasons of uncertainty and healing, and each experience strengthened the roots of this book. That's what The Healthy & Fun Choices® Way is about: choosing awareness over autopilot, curiosity over criticism, truth over pretending, and joy—even when it arrives quietly.

That's what The Healthy & Fun Choices® Way is really about: It's not just a philosophy—it's a daily practice of awareness, curiosity, and creativity. It's learning how to move through life's unpredictable turns with grace and humor. It's choosing fun even when it's hard, because joy itself is a healing force.

This book is proof that we can rebuild from within. When we nurture both the inner and outer parts of ourselves, we open space for others to heal, too. My goal is to create braver spaces—places where people feel safe to learn, to speak, to stretch, and to be fully themselves. Whether in a yoga class, a ski hill huddle, or an everyday conversation, we can all make room for courage and connection. I've lived with many labels—Aphasia, Dyslexia, ADHD, Endometriosis, designer, artist, coach, caregiver, mom, daughter, friend—but I see them now as ingredients, not limits. They remind me how resilient the human spirit is.

With over three decades as a designer, I've built this book to be accessible and visually friendly—short chapters, simple ideas, and stories you can dip into intuitively. Read front to back or skip around. Pause when you need to. Come back when you're ready. Let it be a gentle guide filled with encouragement, clarity, and play.

One afternoon, while finishing this manuscript, I locked myself in my room to focus. Suddenly, I heard a soft tap on the window. A bird—a cedar waxwing with markings that looked like tiny sunglasses—was peering straight at me. I laughed, lifted the blinds, and soon ten more appeared beside it. That moment reminded me: nature is always speaking, guiding, and reminding us to look up.

May this help you pause,
breathe,

    notice the beauty around you,

and rediscover your
    own brilliance—

    one choice,

        one breath,

            one word at a time.

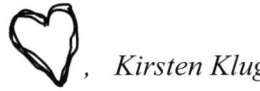, *Kirsten Klug*

Table of Contents

Chapter 1	Embrace the Now	15
Chapter 2	Your Words Matter	25
Chapter 3	Just Add Fun	35
Chapter 4	Lead with Curiosity	39
Chapter 5	Love Yourself More	57
Chapter 6	Honor Your Creativity	65
Chapter 7	Reframe It	71
Chapter 8	Mistakes are Magic	85
Chapter 9	Resiliency for Braver Living	89
Chapter 10	Redefine Healthy	95
Chapter 11	Rest & Restore	103
Chapter 12	Food as Fuel	109
Chapter 13	Eating by Color	117
Chapter 14	Being Proactive Over Reactive	143
Chapter 15	Leading with Intention	147
Chapter 16	Make a Choice!	163
Chapter 17	Functional Fitness & Movement	171
Chapter 18	Healing & Self-care	183
Chapter 19	Yoga is Magic	193
Chapter 20	Just Show Up to Open Up	197
Chapter 21	Leading with Love	203
Chapter 22	Pets as Companions	209
Chapter 23	Nurture Nature	215
Chapter 24	Brilliant You	221
Chapter 25	Just Breathe	229
	About the Author	233

***Sometimes life lessons
show up when you least expect it.
-Kirsten Klug**

Chapter 1
Embrace the Now

Life doesn't usually change in big, dramatic moments. It shifts in the small ones. The moment you pause before reacting. The moment you choose to move your body, even when you don't feel like it. The moment you give yourself permission to laugh, rest, or simply begin again tomorrow.

One of the most powerful moments that taught me how to embrace the now happened unexpectedly, on a cold and rainy President's Day in 2016, when I had gone up to the mountain for ski race training. This experience was probably only about fifteen minutes in length, yet it allowed me use mental, physical and spiritual strength we have available to us. Sometimes life lessons show up when you least expect it.

We went to get on the Stadium chair lift to go up to the top of the ski race training hill, as I was a coach and my son was a racer. Even if you do not ride ski lifts, you can imagine that you wait in line, and when it's your turn, you go out, and sit on the bench of the chair all at the same time— sometimes with people you don't even know.

On this day, as we all sat down to relax and start talking — we all slid off of the seats! As I reached back and pulled myself up, I realized there was a sheet of ice. This was not normal. I reached quickly and grabbed the back of my son's jacket and pulled him up and said, "Hang on to the back of the chair."

Then, I heard a cry for help from the girl on my right. I tried to get her jacket and pull her up, but her hip had slid below the seat. I couldn't get her up. So I said we will call for help and I explained how she could fall into the snow just a couple feet down.

We hollered back for the chairlift operators to stop the chair, but no one was there. I hollered at the other skiers getting on the next chair. I looked down to see that she had landed softly—but I couldn't find her. Swiftly, the chair sped up and went up and up, as we were on a high-speed quad lift. My son yelled, "Mom! She fell, but she's still holding on!"

I looked over the side and realized what had happened. I could relate and my heart sunk! She was too afraid to fall all the way or her hand had gotten stuck. I threw my poles to the ground, reached over the side of the chair, and grabbed her hands. Our eyes were glued to each other and my arms were fully extended as she dangled in mid air off the side of the express ski lift. It went up and up and up!

"Just hold on," I yelled as I tightened my grip on her wet gloves. I continued to shout for help to the chairlifts behind us and told my son to hold on tighter.

Finally, the chair stopped at the third riblet—we were 30 feet up! Time stood still for a moment as we realized what had just happened. I took a deep breath and in that moment knew I would not let these kids face fear alone.

I heard the girl, "What if I die? What if I can't hold on and I slip and fall?" I looked her right in the eyes and said, "I've got you. You are not going to fall. We are going to hold on until help comes. There's got to be a way."

It all happened quickly, and decisions had to be made. Feeling the gravity tugging at my shoulders, I asked her how old she was and it turned out my son and her were the same age. I told them they are the two strongest 8-year-olds I know. Our chit chat continued to keep us entertained.

Determined in my responses, I knew that even in the most challenging moment of my life, we could overcome this ordeal. I decided to focus on the present moment intensely.

"We will survive, and by working together, we can do this!" I proclaimed. As fatigue began to set in, I employed an intermittent holding technique—similar to what I used in spin classes when my legs grew weary. I explained it as we tried it: we tightened our grip with one hand while briefly relieving the other, then switched. I realized we could count down, like in ski racing, to stay focused: Together out loud, we counted "5-4-3-2-1."

It helped us know when to switch our grip. Our plan worked. We took deep breaths and stayed completely focused.

When it was hard, we leaned in and addressed the situation. We could even feel nature around us had shifted. The wind had stopped and the sun came out. Between our counting down we shared hopeful ideas like that the bird could just fly her down safely. At one point my son was making plans on how we could climb down the pole. All of our little talk helped lessen the load on our minds, yet our arms were aching and we could feel the sweat and tears.

Eventually, help arrived from below with a tarp, and I was advised to let go of her hands. It was a tough decision, as I had no idea whether she would live or succumb to the fall. We looked at each other and I said, "we have to let go." She hit the tarp with skis on. After a few minutes she was able to stand up and walk away. Her parents were there and she looked to be okay.

My son and I sat on the chairlift, upset and expressing our frustration. "Why did this happen? How could we move forward? What now?" We were discussing the scenarios. We were both very angry, relieved she got up and walked and I had a lot of pain, but chose to not reveal that now.

At the top as we got off the chairlift I trembled with emotion, and after speaking with the ski area, checking on the girl's condition and checking in with my boss, I found out that they didn't really want us around.

In fact, there was a concern that I had caused the accident. It was so far from the truth. It gave me a chance to talk to my son about how high emotions can cause misunderstanding.

We realized that this can be the unfortunate part of caring. I was emotionally exhausted and my shoulder and arm were very sore. My son said he really didn't want to train in the rain, anyways. We sat in the car and took some deep breaths before traveling home for an hour.

Later that night I wrote a letter and followed up with exactly what happened. The three of us from Chairlift 11 have a strong understanding of what it takes to persevere—emotionally, physically and spiritually. The next weekend, both kids did great at their races and still to this day they lead their high school ski race teams and, I still coach, almost ten years later.

That experience profoundly allowed me to realize that the philosophies I had shared with so many others were useful in the most dire situations, too. Our ability to stay very present and focused was key. Keeping our communication uplifting with ideas and solutions was hopeful. Trying new approaches with creativity let us get through, even when it was super hard.

Following up with kindness for myself, my son and others was essential. I felt it was really important to get information out to the ski team and ski area about what happened and how it can be better prevented. All ski areas need lift operators at the chair lift to ensure skiers get on fine. All skiers need pole straps off of their wrists upon getting on the lift. Looking back, I am so thankful of our positive outcome.

The next day I went for a walk with my dog at a park nearby. I tried to do more relaxing activities in order to calm my mind and my arms, which were still flustered. I met a person walking their dog—who also happened to be the same breed as my dog, a French Brittany. Our dogs looked like they could be sisters.

Upon asking more, we found out they had the same parents and were most likely related. I asked her what her dog's name was, and she said, "YOLO." What an experience—to live in the moment one day and then the next day be reminded by a dog named YOLO. It was even on the wall of our gym, but it had never truly resonated with me until that moment.

YOLO is an acronym for You Only Live Once: so make the most of it. The rest of my walk I pondered…"Was I making the most of my life today?" And maybe that's a question for you too—are you making the most of today?

You might quickly think of your accomplishments, your relationships, or even your work.

You might also notice a gap, something you'd like to shift. I had great ideas. I thought deeper: 'I had developed the educational program Healthy & Fun Choices™ and been sharing it with thousands of school kids and large organizations. We had designed and built our dream home, even though we felt it was too big. We had wonderful kids and parents nearby. I was currently an Assistant Guide at a Montessori school and Camp Director. I had been a graphic designer, business owner, and speaker.' Still, I asked myself, "Am I doing all that I can to help others, my family, or myself?"

What would your answer be?

Little Choices Can Lead to Connection & Perspective
These little choices may seem ordinary, but they are powerful. They shape how we feel, how we connect, and how we live.

The Healthy & Fun Choices Way is about noticing them and choosing actions, words, and perspectives that bring more joy, less stress, and deeper connection.

When most people hear the word healthy, they picture a number on a scale, a workout routine, or a perfect plate of food. But that definition is far too small. To me, "healthy" means being present. It means finding joy in the everyday, choosing kindness over judgment, curiosity over fear, resilience over perfection.

When It All Adds Up
That realization didn't come all at once—it grew from my own journey. When I first started living on my own in college, I had a real shock. Suddenly, food and ice cream were available whenever I wanted, and there were no strict sports schedules like in high school. I quickly realized it wasn't what my body needed as my endometriosis pain increased and my energy decreased. Not what I needed for ski racing, where agility and speed are essential. When dry-land training started in October, it was an eye opener—if I wanted to perform well, I needed to schedule time to work out, eat well, and take care of myself.

That focus on self-care paid off: our girls' ski team made it to Regionals in Winterpark, Colorado—a moment that really showed me how important my dedication to whole health and balance was for now and the future.

Noticing how I felt more alive and setting an example for others as one of the coaches made staying dedicated to healthy and fun choices, important. That was really the birth of Healthy & Fun Choices for me—learning how to balance freedom with responsibility, and discovering that health isn't just about rules, it's about choices, fun, and curiosity. Our health is about worrying less about did we do this or that right or wrong.

Throughout college, I continued to ski race, but I also decided to be playful and try different activities where I could make friends and challenge myself to just show up, regardless of pain. That spring, I joined the crew team and learned how effort can appear in beautiful quiet moments—experiencing the fog lift on a lake with mountain views appearing in the distance. From intramural soccer to being a radio personality, working as a barista at a coffee shop with friends, I explored ways to push myself creatively and socially. At the same time, I studied graphic design and printing and publishing arts, which taught me how to face challenges and creatively figure out next steps.

Double Vision

I call this approach "Double Vision"—seeing the big picture while also attending to the small details. That's what life and our health are all about: the big picture is wanting to live a long, healthy life, and the small details are being present and making choices today that benefit us always.

Of course, changes happen that you don't expect—in college my oboe teacher passed away and he was my hero. I also lost friends at the end of high school in unfortunate accidents. I got pretty depressed and sometimes let my endometriosis pain really set in. Learning how to pick yourself back up and finding support to get through, is a critical part of the journey.

At the same time, I noticed that most people still judged health only by appearance. If someone was overweight, they were assumed unhealthy; if too thin, something was "wrong." I knew there was more to the story.

Around that same time, I began noticing something important about health care settings. My dad was an orthodontist, and I worked in his practice during summers, but it wasn't until I was a graphic designer and started helping with his logo design, marketing, and educational materials that I realized dentists and orthodontists often had something doctors don't—extra time with their patients.

That insight sparked a bigger idea: I could help dentists integrate and educate patients about the whole health concepts in addition to the dental health because it all goes together. Dentists loved the ideas! From there, my work expanded quickly. After starting my graphic design agency in 1994, ID Graphics, my business partner and I worked with 75 dental clients over fifteen years, as well as businesses in other industries—sewing retail, farming, manufacturing, health care, city planners and so on—helping them create programs, campaigns, and experiences that brought the Healthy & Fun Choices way subtly into the lives of their staff and patients/customers.

I also found ways to bring these ideas into unexpected places. With sewing retailers, for example, I helped them invite customers to gather over quilting and sewing projects—not just to buy a sewing machine or make something beautiful, but to connect, share community, and find joy in giving handmade gifts. I developed campaigns that encouraged people to celebrate their creativity, and worked with businesses to bring healthy and fun choices into staff programs. For some, that even led to shortened work weeks for rest and recharge. A shift began: people started expanding their idea of what "healthy" really means.

One day, we were interviewing a client whose third-generation family business we had helped rebuild after a major fire and they lost of everything. I expected him to mention the marketing campaigns or the realignment of his budgets—but instead, he said something that inspired me: "Working with you has allowed me to have less stress, more joy, and, more time with my family."

That moment revealed to me what healthy really means. It's not just about strategies or outcomes—it's about creating braver space for connection, presence, and joy. And just as I encouraged others to embrace this broader vision of health, I had to navigate my own challenges with habits, cravings, and coping strategies.

Living a healthy and fun life requires daily intention, a mindset that focuses on growth, awareness, and the choices that truly support our long-term well-being.

I reflected on why I had traded my business ownership job for that of teaching in upper elementary and that was because I wanted to learn more about how we learn. That's when I realized life's purpose isn't always flashy. Sometimes it's quiet and reflective—like that moment on the lift when presence was everything.

Because here's the truth: it's not enough to hear "You Got This!" We have to live it. We have to choose—moment by moment—what will help us feel fully alive today and shape the legacy we want to leave.

That's what this book is about. My hope is that you will find Your Healthy & Fun Choices Way, an invitation that inspires you to explore your ideas, stories, and actions—and see how the words, thoughts, and choices you make can transform both your present and your future.

In my opinion, the best way isn't just to read about it or listen to the audio book—it is also to experience what it means for you. You will find ideas and activities within this book and I challenge you to try them on.

Sometimes the big concept of "what do I want to focus on to get to where I want to go" is hard. So instead I say focus on what you are wanting to do today. How do you define your YOLO?

Filing Up Your Container
There is a story about a professor who fills a container up with rocks. The bigger ones have to go in first, then the medium sized ones and then the small ones. I like to think about life as a container of rocks—the big ones are your top priorities, the medium ones important, the small ones little things that you can do each day to help you feel alive.

24   *The Healthy & Fun Choices Way*

What are your rocks?

If you were to write out or draw a container and fill it with rocks, what does YOLO mean to you today?

Maybe you can write it out, or get a container and find your rocks and each of the big ones write a label them.

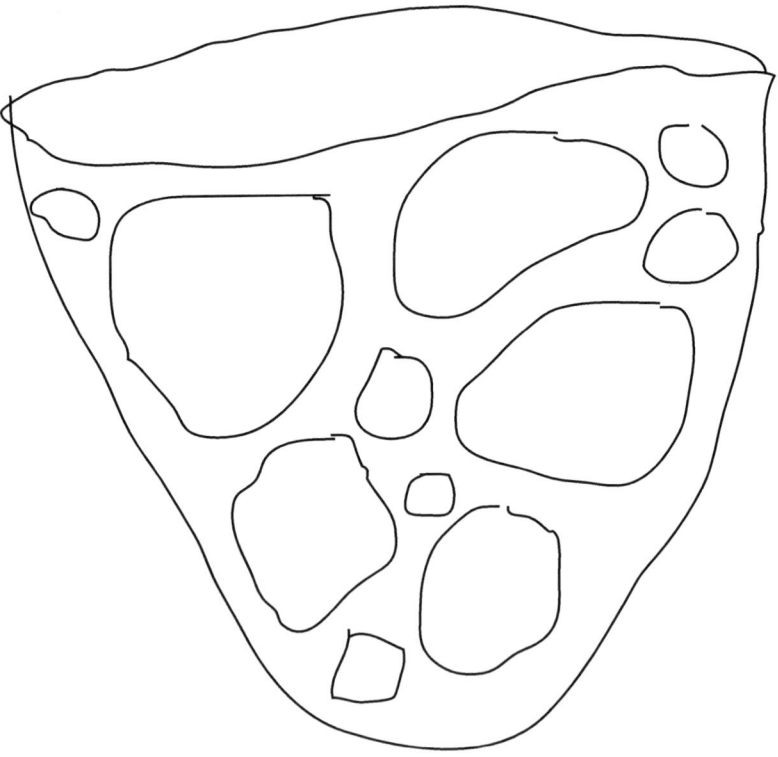

Chapter 2

Your Words Matter

How we experience life isn't just about what we do—it's also shaped by the words we say to ourselves, the words we allow from others, and the way we react when something comes out differently than intended.

People with Aphasia often get frustrated when the words don't land quite right. A quick sigh, a "gah," or a playful slap to the forehead can show up in those moments. But even without Aphasia, the same patterns happen. Words carry emotion, and the way we use or respond to them can either drag us down or lift us up.

Our words and gestures matter—whether spoken aloud or whispered inside the mind. The background chatter, the second-guessing, those "I am" statements and quiet affirmations all have energy. The inner dialogue and stories we tell ourselves can shape how we show up in the world. They can build confidence or slowly erode it.

Words influence everything—from the soft murmur of self-talk to the voices around us, to the lyrics in a song, or even the silence between moments. Becoming aware of that influence helps us understand how words shape feelings and actions.

Imagine being in a store trying on a shirt. The mirror reflects not just an image but a thought: "Oh, I like these colors" or "Ugh, this doesn't look good on me." Ask a friend, "What do you think?" and their response—"Looks great!" or "That's not flattering"—can shift the mood instantly. Tone, volume, facial expression—all play a role in what we feel remember.

My birthday falls just after Christmas, so shopping and lunch with my parents has been a long-standing tradition. It's something to look forward to—our little post-holiday ritual. Later, when married, my mother-in-law began inviting me out before the holidays because she had special coupons. What should have been fun often left me depleted and sad afterward. It's not an easy story to tell, because those outings hurt for many years, even though her son encouraged me to go—after all, it was free clothing and time with his mom.

One year, the kids came along. They were old enough to notice how she spoke to me, the little jabs and criticisms tucked into her comments. My son grew upset and started crying; my daughter stomped toward the exit, declaring we were leaving. That was the last time we went shopping together.

Much of that marriage was filled with put-downs followed by my attempts to smooth things over—negative words met with problem-solving, criticism met with optimism. Sometimes the back-and-forth turned into arguments because both sides carried truth, but our reactions were toxic. Eventually, it became clear that not every battle needed to be fought. Boundaries had to be set, and so did a bit of tongue-biting. Sometimes kindness meant saying less.

Thinking about those boundaries brings up a completely different memory—music class in sixth grade. Back then, playing the flute felt fun but also competitive. One day, the band teacher mentioned his best friend, an oboe teacher. He said, "The oboe is a difficult and beautiful instrument, and I think you can handle it." That simple statement sparked curiosity.

A visit to Bob Scott's house the following weekend changed everything. Listening to him play the oboe was mesmerizing. Bob had a warmth and patience that made learning feel like discovery. He said, "The best part about the oboe is that because it's so hard, you'll make mistakes." When asked, "So… making mistakes is good?" He leaned in and smiled.

"Yes. Listen to this—and learn how to turn those mistakes into magic."

That phrase stuck. The oboe became part of my life for nine years, with plenty of squeaks, laughter, and progress. Sophomore year, the band won State, and during a big solo, there were a few missteps—but they blended right into the music. No one knew.

Bob passed away while I was in college, but his wisdom continues to echo. He taught why fun, words, and our approach to challenges are the true keys to joy.

The Paper People© exercise is part of the Healthy & Fun Choices® workshops. It's a reminder that words really do matter, and that with practice, laughter, and perspective, even mistakes can become magic.

Up & Aware©

Sad Soul©

Exercise #1: PAPER PEOPLE

Above is Sad Soul© sitting with head down. Up & Aware© with arms out wide ready to take on anything. We are going to do an activity with the two drawings above that represent how we feel when we hear different words or phrases.

Directions:
1. Get each character on its own page—you can copy them and cut them out or simply redraw them on two different pieces of paper.

2. Take the paper with Sad Soul© on it and imagine negative and rude words and phrases that you say to yourself or you have heard people say to you/others.

3. Say those phrases out loud and fold the pager in half with the Sad Soul© on the inside. Keep going until the paper is small and scrunched up. Examples: "I don't like you." "Your shoes are not as nice as mine." "You aren't smart enough." "You are ugly and fat."

4. Notice how closed up Sad Soul© character is after hearing all those sayings and getting scrunched up. Set Sad Soul© scrunched up aside.

5. Take your separate paper with Up & Aware© on it.

6. Draw stars or put sticker stars around the outside of the character as you say statements like "I like you" "You are kind." "You are creative and fun!" "Your laughter makes me smile." "You have a nice way about you."

7. Add a smiley face. Notice how Up and Aware© this drawing is and how happy you feel just looking at it.

Doing this exercise with the Paper People© might seem silly at first, but as you participate you can really get the polarity of what happens with us in how we can move through life thinking that things are good or bad, right or wrong, enough or not enough.

When leading workshops at schools, universities or in business conferences, students get very enthusiastic about sharing words and phrases. There are groups who stomp or crease down the folding of Sad Soul© and there are groups that glow while hearing the joy from Up & Aware© statements that are shared. Everyone relates to how these statements make us feel.

There are times when we can sit with Sad Soul©, but it's not helpful for us to be there all the time. Same with Up & Aware©.

Keep that Up & Aware© Paper Person standing up or maybe even tape it to the side of where you are reading or slip it into the front of the book. Here you can see how our words and actions can keep us standing and open.

Set that crumpled paper of Sad Soul© next to it. Maybe you can relate to Sad Soul©, when we put ourselves down or allow others to. We can feel like a crumpled up piece of paper. But you don't have to be that way forever, feelings are temporary and can adjust as we learn and notice the warnings.

Now, reflect a little bit about what YOU felt doing this little exercise or what concerns bubble up:

Exercise #2: CREATIVE YOU
See the illustration on this page and refer to the descriptions here for each section.

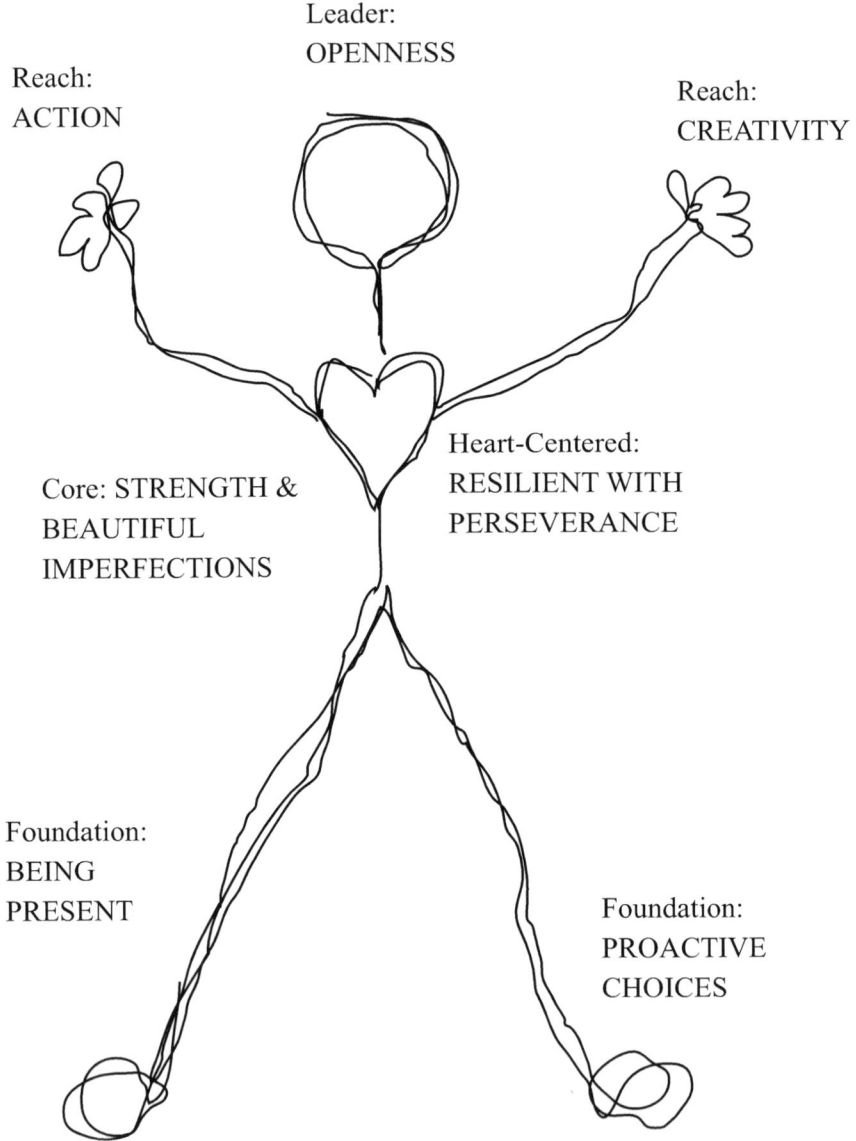

Leader: OPENNESS
What do you want to think about and be inspired by? What do you want to see, hear, taste, smell, and touch?

Reach: ACTION
How can you move forward in action? What are you doing today, like reading this book, that will help you keep moving forward?

Reach: CREATIVITY
What is the perspective you need? What gifts do you love about yourself right now? What would you like to learn?

Foundation: BEING PRESENT
What do you want to be known for? What are you doing right now and what do you want in the future?

Foundation: PROACTIVE CHOICES
What actions could you take today that would help you reach your vision? Who do you want to surround yourself with?

Core: STRENGTH & IMPERFECTIONS
What are your imperfections and how can you witness them as beautiful? Where are your strengths and weaknesses?

Heart-Centered: RESILIENT PERSEVERANCE

What would it feel like if you could lead with your heart? How can you make changes that are in line with loving yourself more? Please note: You can redraw the stick figure on another page or create a person out of a wire. There is no right or wrong—this is just a fun idea and an ability for us to think about what it is that makes you, YOU.

Through these exercises, you might start noticing the words you say to yourself in your self-talk, as well as how you talk about yourself to others.

Sometimes, joking around about your imperfections can help you feel lighter and take life a little less seriously. At the same time, it's worth paying attention to how others respond—and to your own feelings—so you can be kind to yourself and those around you. From my experience, our brains tend to focus more on negative words or put-downs than on the laughter, so a little awareness goes a long way.

It can be helpful to practice speaking to yourself with kindness, both in your inner voice and out loud. Instead of saying, "oops, dumb me," you might try, "oh, what I meant to say was…" or "next time I can try ___." Small shifts like this can make a big difference in how you experience your day.

The way we see ourselves and the choices we make all connect. The more we can let go of mistakes and learn from them, the more we can create a life we love and enjoy the process of building it. Holding onto frustration or pain can sometimes lead us to seek comfort in less helpful ways, like unhealthy food, addictions or distractions. Awareness helps us notice these moments and choose differently.

All our words and actions fit together like pieces of a puzzle, shaping our lives one choice at a time.

We start this book by exploring feelings, thoughts, words, and actions because awareness is the key to showing up as you want. The more we notice and reflect, the more space we create to be kind—to ourselves, to others, and to our creative process. I call these words "More Time to..." Words because by focusing on words, stories and ideas that allow us to be with our happy or joyful parts, *we actually find more time* on what we like. It's such a simple practice and yet we forget how easy this can be.

What words resonate with you the most from this list below?

What stories pop up when you think about the words?

JOY	LAUGHTER	SUNSHINE
GRIT	DETERMINATION	RESILIENCE
PRESENT	GROWTH	CREATIVITY
INTUITION	AWARENESS	ACTION
PEACE	MINDFUL	REACH
BRAVER	IMAGINE	FLOW
BREATHE	DREAM	LEADERSHIP

Use this space for reflection or write down other words that you like...

Our Words and Actions become our seeds of reflections of growth.
-Kirsten Klug

Chapter 3

Just Add Fun

Big or little changes and transitions can make life challenging at times. Every day can look different, and adjusting to what life throws at us—or what we expect of ourselves—can feel heavy.

When life gets overwhelming, I've learned that adding fun can make everything lighter. Fun doesn't erase the challenges, but it gives us energy, creativity, and a way to keep moving. Sometimes it's as simple as laughing with a friend, sometimes it's about trying something new, and sometimes it's choosing to see a situation in a playful way instead of a pressured one.

One of my favorite examples of this came from working with my friend, Ayse, who had a massive AVM stroke and developed aphasia and apraxia. For a whole year, the only word she could say was "no." I understood her struggle deeply because during my own hospitalization, "no" was the only word I could say for a time too. Years later, we met in an Aphasia Ambassador group, and even though her speech was still limited, we discovered a fun way to work together. She wanted to share her story, so we created a slideshow presentation.

She picked the colors, gathered the photos, and even when words were hard, she found ways to communicate with sticky notes and gestures. I brought my design skills, and together we built something beautiful. What surprised me most was how much fun we had while doing it. We laughed, we experimented, and by the end, we weren't just creating a presentation—we were creating joy. That joy has carried us into more projects, videos with other Aphasia speaking opportunities, and hopefully more!

That experience reminded me that fun isn't just about play—it's a spark. It gives us motivation, connection, and courage.

I've found the same thing in my yoga community. I teach yoga to show that there's no perfect way to hold a pose—or to be here in the world. We can fall out, get back up, notice thoughts and let them go, and return to the breath. Moving through uncertainty, we feel the flow between poses instead of staying rigid. Yoga invites us to experiment, to play, and to approach ourselves with curiosity rather than judgment.

Last year, a group of us decided to learn how to play Mahjong. None of us knew what we were doing, but it was such a challenge and so much fun that we've now played almost every Saturday since. What started as a game has turned into deep friendship—we share photos, jokes, little daily wins, and encouragement with each other.

Fun has also shown up in unexpected places. At a Love Your Brain retreat, my roommates and I bonded over a string of funny moments—like when a roommate who is blind realized too late that she had hung her clothes on hooks right in the shower spray, leaving her with nothing dry to wear. I offered her a swimsuit. We laughed until tears came, and what could have been frustrating turned into great friendships. Because those moments of fun built a lasting bond.

Even nature has its way of reminding us to lighten up. In 2023, while planning a memorial for my business coach, Dr. Thomas Jones, I walked under a big oak tree. A squirrel dropped an acorn right at my feet. When I picked it up, I noticed it looked like a little person wearing a ski hat, and it instantly made me smile. Later, when I found a tiny oak tree sprouting in my yard, I realized it was a lesson: fun and curiosity plant seeds that grow into something bigger.

One of my favorite lessons in this season came during a retreat. A counselor invited us to get up early and hike to see the sunrise. But when we got to the lookout, the sun was hidden. At first, it felt like a disappointment—like we'd come up short. But then I realized that the whole point wasn't the sunrise at all. Even our leader allowed us to sit with that concept for a moment. It was the being together, the walk, the stillness, and the moment.

Life is like that, too. We don't always get the "view" we expect, but we do get the experience. And that is where courage lives—in the willingness to be present, even when things don't go as planned. That's where fun comes in, too. Fun is brave because it allows us to release the pressure of performance, achievement, or perfection. Fun reminds us that we're not here just to "win the race" or "get to heaven"—we're here to be here now. To breathe, to laugh, to connect, to cherish the good and the hard. Even with disabilities, we still hold abilities. Even with shortcomings, we still have opportunities to find peace in the moment. I invite you to pause just now, inhale and exhale.

Here's the truth: fun changes everything. It boosts our energy and creativity, lowers stress, and helps us connect more deeply with others. Neuroscience even shows that when we're having fun, our brains release dopamine, making it easier to learn, remember, and stay motivated. In other words—fun isn't extra, it's essential.

Coaching the ski team has been another powerful reminder of this. We focus on speed, yes, but we also focus on fun—because fun unlocks performance. My athletes don't just race gates; they ski backwards, create human bobsleds, and try silly tricks. They laugh on the chairlifts, share stories, and build community on the mountain. And yet, because they approach the hill with joy, they ski faster, cleaner, and with more energy. They've learned that fun doesn't take away from excellence—it fuels it.

When my kids were younger, we had something we called Fun Fridays. A group of moms and kids would meet every Friday to do something playful together—going to the zoo, exploring a park, visiting the children's museum, or heading to the beach. It was as life-giving for us moms as it was for the kids. While the kids played, we compared notes, shared struggles, and swapped solutions. It was a reminder that fun builds not only joy but also community, perspective, and support.

See what comes up when you look at your own life:
- What activities bring you joy and fun right now?
- Who could you invite over to cook, play, or laugh with?
- Where might you add a little playfulness into your day?

Fun doesn't erase pain or challenges, but it transforms how we move through them. It allows us to see possibilities instead of only problems. And most importantly, it reminds us that we're alive—that life is meant to be lived, not just endured.

Just add fun. And watch what grows.

Chapter 4

Lead with Curiosity

Sometimes life throws curve balls, and the first reaction is frustration, stress, or even defeat. But when those moments are met with curiosity, something shifts—it softens the pressure and opens the door to new possibilities.

As a graphic designer and strategist, clients often brought complex challenges or creative roadblocks. Rather than rushing to fix things, the best results came from staying present, asking questions, and experimenting with playful ideas. That approach not only improved our conversations but shaped creativity in powerful ways. It's a practice that influences change.

To show how curiosity can unlock bigger outcomes, here are a few real-world examples from clients and projects I designed. Each began with questions, collaboration, and a willingness to explore what might be possible.

Educate First for the Bigger Picture
In the late 1990s, a friend's father discovered a small electric vehicle called the S-Lem at the World's Fair and hoped to import it to the United States. These vehicles were far ahead of their time—too fast and heavy for bike paths, yet too small and short-ranged for traditional roads. Most people simply didn't understand where they fit.

Instead of focusing solely on import logistics, I realized the opportunity lay in education. The challenge became helping consumers, government officials, and the auto industry envision how these vehicles could fill a unique gap in transportation. Working together we decided auto shows and drag races could be the stage for conversations/demonstration. People were intrigued.

Manufacturers paid attention. Our simple S-Lem Flier and playful conversations helped spark a shift in how electric vehicles were perceived—long before "EV" became a household term.

Look Beyond What Isn't Available
Around the same time, a client who developed properties in Portland expressed frustration that there was "nowhere left to build." During a meeting, that comment brought to mind a sign spotted earlier across from another client's building downtown—one that read "Unbuildable."

That word wouldn't leave the mind, so a question was asked: "What about the land marked unbuildable?" Together, maps were pulled out and possibilities were circled. That simple exchange with developer Mark became part of the early brainstorming that helped transform a once-forgotten area into what is now known as the Pearl District—proof that a single curious question can change a cityscape.

Turn Obstacles into Opportunity
Liepold Farms came looking for a new logo design to attract more visitors. At the time, people were flocking to big-box stores instead of family farms. Through conversation, it became clear to me that they needed more than just a logo—I explained that they needed a conversation starter like a brochure and an experience on the farm to reconnect people to the land.

The brochure encouraged conversations for local deliveries and ways that restaurants could get their organic berries. The logo was put on shirts and signs went up advertising the local Harvest Festival.

The idea of a Harvest Festival emerged: tractor rides, food, and entertainment that would celebrate local agriculture. The owners hesitated at first—they didn't even grow pumpkins!

But brainstorming continued, exploring how to partner with other nearby farms and even start city farmers' markets to bring produce closer to consumers.

Those playful ideas took root. Today, the Liepold Farms Harvest Festival draws lots and lots of visitors each year, the farmers' markets now are run by the cities and they thrive across the region. A creative conversation turned into a legacy of community and connection. Their berries are still featured in restaurant foods, like Burgervilles' shakes!

Redefining Dreams Even After Loss
To lose a business or a home to fire is devastating. When we started working with Montavilla Sewing Centers, a sewing retailer, we realized it wasn't just another ad design promoting sewing machines that would draw people in after losing everything. It was time to reconnect with their customers and neighbors in an even bigger way. Leaning in and asking the owners "What is it exactly that you want?" led to a realization that if they were going to rebuild one store, they wanted to expand and have stores in multiple locations. And they wanted their customers to see them as a place to gather, rather than just a store. To do so, communication in finding out where customers lived was key.

We started a website, videos and an ad campaign that featured stories about projects their customers were making for others, we designed conversation starters and had the sales team ask more questions. Through the conversations we featured ways that customers could come in to be part of the sewing community with classes and clubs, instead of just buying a machine.

The conversations led to communications, stories and ideas that created a wonderful brand and, yes, five stores and all community-based for sewers to come in and enjoy classes, clubs and events. Machine sales were up, too!

Innovation in the Display
While I was sitting in the waiting room at a client who manufactured hanging hardware, the receptionist seemed upset after opening a box. She looked over at me and said if there is any way you could make it so our product samples actually get to the clients, that would be amazing. So I got up and walked over and we started looking at how they had been sending out samples and what th problems were.

Through our conversations, I decided to ask the owner if we could come up with a solution. He said 'Yes!" We came back with a box design that held the products in place and had a brochure integrated into it explaining more about the products. After little adjustments here and there we had a final sample box and started sending them out to clients and retailers.

What happened next, we didn't expect... instead of just demonstrating the products, the clients and used the display box in the store and it increase products sales immensely!

How One Practice Sparked an Industry Shift
Our work in dental and orthodontic marketing began with one simple idea: practices thrive when they build relationships rooted in community, not self-promotion. As my father prepared to open his new office, we renamed the practice to reflect the neighborhood—Sunnyside Orthodontic Specialists—and created campaigns that were fresh, memorable, and truly helpful to nearby dentists. Instead of the standard referral gifts, we designed educational calendars, creative mailers, and connection-focused marketing that people actually looked forward to receiving. The approach caught on fast. Within a short time, more than fifty practices adopted our methods, shifting the industry toward more authentic, integrity-based communication.

The Joy of Learning Through Play

During the years when my kids were young, summer camps became another outlet for this same philosophy. Rather than just having a camp that offered art, science or legos. I decided to create camps where I could share ideas and the campers could take the Healthy & Fun Choices© ideas into interactive learning and hands-on exploration.

Kids created recipes, went grocery shopping, cooked meals, created dream boats that set sail in local streams, and sculpted clay toothbrush holders or strawberry planters. At one 4-H camp, children worked alongside their dogs at the old Alpenrose Dairy farm. Another camp paired morning gardening with afternoon harvesting; the students sold their products at their very own mini farmers' market by week's end. Some even created their own herbal teas—growing, drying, and packaging them.

Years later, parents still share how much their children remember those camps. That joy in learning stuck because fun creates curiosity leading to strong memories.

This same principle shines through in the Healthy & Fun Choices® school programs. In a single one-hour workshop filled with hands-on, playful learning, students absorbed powerful messages about health, choices, and joy.

Immediately afterward, they remembered every detail. A year later, they still remembered. Even five or ten years down the road, former students could describe the concepts—and many said they'd used them in daily life to make positive choices.

That's the magic of combining fun with meaning. A single hour of joyful learning can leave an imprint that lasts a lifetime.

Why Fun Strengthens Memory

Research backs up what those experiences proved: dopamine—the brain's "feel-good" chemical—supports memory formation.

When we do something enjoyable or new, dopamine floods the system, enhancing learning and recall.

Novelty also deepens retention. Scientists have found two dopamine-based systems in the brain: one activates when something feels familiar, and the other when something feels completely new. Both help the hippocampus—the memory center—store experiences more vividly.

Even small, practical tricks can make remembering easier. For instance, taking a quick selfie with a new acquaintance and texting it to them with both names attached helps anchor the connection. Seeing the image again later reinforces the memory through repetition and association.

What techniques do you use to remember names or faces? Put simply: when something is fun, fresh, or emotionally engaging, dopamine locks the memory in and makes it easier to recall later.

Challenges and Fun Go Hand in Hand
Here's the thing—challenges and fun aren't opposites. In fact, they can work together. Sometimes the harder the challenge, the more important it is to add fun in the moment. Fun shifts the energy, brings people together, and makes tasks feel lighter.

That's exactly what I discovered when creating the Healthy & Fun Choices workshops. We didn't just sit and talk—we stayed active, grouping students into teams and explaining each challenge as we went. They watched, learned, and supported one another. Instead of racing for speed, the goal was completing tasks together and cheering teammates on. Students planned strategies, helped each other solve tricky moments, and celebrated every success. Even classes with diverse abilities integrated easily, and every student felt included.

The winners weren't the ones who finished fastest. The winners were the ones who all participated—because participation is what creates connection. Every single student, all 10,000 of them over quite a few years got involved, because it wasn't about perfection, it was about play. And the teachers brought the ideas back to the classroom and the activity books that I had designed bridged the gaps and brought the ideas home. The conversations continued beyond the first workshop experience. The whole package created an unforgettable experience.

One of the most powerful activities in the hands-on workshop was the "banana relay race." Each team had to do funny exercises and challenges while balancing a banana (but not with their hand) that represented themselves. They had to try not to squish it. They did a variety of relays from bunny hops to crab walks, picking up the laundry that we would drop along the path, scooting on a 4-wheel scooter down and back, cheering on their teammates, and brushing the teeth of a stuffed animal while the walked down and back. At the end of all the relay races, I opened one of the bananas to show how, on the outside, everything looked fine, but on the inside, it was bruised. We can look "fine" on the outside, but sometimes inside we're carrying stress, sadness, or pain.

At the end of the relays, we went back to the Paper People© activity, just like how this book started in Chapter 2. I held up the two pieces of paper so the kids saw how the Sad Soul© stayed folded and closed up, and how Up & Aware© was the one that took it all in—the part of us that can actually experience change. Then I asked them, "What can we do?"

Without hesitation, the kids shouted back: "Add Fun!"

And when I asked, "What do we need to do to really open up?" They yelled even louder: "Show up to open up!" ***That's the heart of it.*** When we're present in the moment, when we bring fun into our challenges, when we're willing to have conversations, ask questions and show up with openness—we discover that anything is possible. What is amazing to me, even ten years later after a person had attended the workshop and they see me, they can still recall the message and often share parts of what they really enjoyed and took with them for life!

Reflective Takeaway
What I've learned through all of this is that fun isn't just about laughter—it's actually a key that can unlock healing, growth, and connection. Challenges will always be part of life, and we can add fun!

If you did the exercise at the beginning of this book with your own Sad Soul© and Up & Aware©, maybe this is the moment to notice how you can start to open it up.

Take a moment here and get present. What has been going well? What is your Up & Aware© Person seeing and experiencing? What could they share with you or with others? Now get your scrunched up Sad Soul© - can you witness how it was closed and didn't see much. Go ahead and open it up!

For me, that shift has been everything. Adding fun, even going through difficult injuries, career shifts, a redefining of family and even selling a dream house, has allowed me to heal, to grow, and to feel more alive. My hope is that as you move forward, you'll see that you don't have to wait until life gets easier to begin. You can choose fun now. In that choice, you may just find the strength, healing, and connection you've been looking for.

Noticing my reflection now, so many years later, I realize just how impactful all of this has been. I feel like you'll want to hear more—about what I shared, the experiences we created, and the ways these stories can show us how fun, connection, and presence can truly transform our choices and our lives.

The Start of New Pathways

At one of my favorite workshops, I partnered with the Boys & Girls Club in Salem. The gym was packed with 350 students, buzzing with energy. I spoke to all of them first, and then with the Director's help, I selected 30 students to come down and participate in the relay races. We formed six teams of five, performing in the middle while the rest of the kids filled the bleachers. We divided the bleachers into the same six teams so that every student could cheer and encourage their teammates, even if they weren't acting it out. The energy was electric—loud, joyful, and energetic.

We did our activities and that banana relay race. I also challenged the students to think differently about the healthy choices they were making. I advised: drink water first before soda or caffeinated drinks. Get outside for walks or play with their pets. If indoors was best, run laps around the couch between video game levels or do ten push-ups after a win and after a loss. What could have been chores or lessons became a game—and a fun, motivating one at that.

A month later, I was invited back for another workshop focused on conversations—how to start talking even when you didn't know what to say. The students split into small groups and created skits, live shows, and question games to entertain all of us. We had break out rooms, too, for kids that didn't want to play large. Their creativity amazed me, and the confidence they built was something they could carry home.

After one of those workshops, a mom came up to me with happy tears in her eyes. She shared that her son had inspired the whole family to switch from soda to water for a month. The family had come from an area where drinking water wasn't safe. So not only did they start feeling better, but they saved enough money to take their very first trip to the Oregon coast. She described walks on the beach, shared laughter, and her son volunteering to take the garbage out and walk the dog. His perspective on life had shifted, and she cried as she thanked me for what she thought was "just a workshop."

Soon, I was invited into other schools and organizations. In Gladstone School District, the entire elementary school participated during their PE classes. Students came up with additional ideas and soon they got salad bars in their lunch room! Together, we created memories the students still talk about today.

At Portland Public Schools, one teacher liked the workshops so much that she had me come back every week to her classroom for six weeks. It was heartwarming to get to know the students, create entertaining activities, and make memories I'm sure they still carry today. Students said things like: "Remember when we wrote a song about the colors of the rainbow in food choices!" or "Remember when we made toothbrush holders out of clay, but instead of a boring box, our holders were characters with big eyes that I still use today!"

At North Clackamas Schools, the workshops expanded into elementary, middle school leadership classes, and science and art projects. One teacher commented on how accessible the program was, noting that students who were autistic, had cerebral palsy, or other disabilities could participate alongside able-bodied peers. She said that ability to include everyone was a true testament that Healthy and Fun Choices™ is for all students.

For a couple of years, I realized the program could be integrated into field days for Portland Public Schools. So reaching out to the Portland Timbers, I was able to get some of the players to help interact with the students playing soccer or even jump rope competitions. Every student received a small activity workbook to take home for the summer, with soccer player signatures inside—a memorable way to continue the lessons.

I had dreamed big about a whole health education event. It became a reality when the Portland Timbers and Providence Health teamed up to host a massive health event at Providence Park, bringing together kids from across Portland Public Schools. Students were fully engaged with fun activities and health lessons before the soccer game. My kids and I had the joy of teaching dance moves with Timber Joey to the entire stadium audience while upbeat songs played for a few years.

Over the loudspeakers, they said, "And here is how to make healthy and fun choices!" A single idea could ripple out.

Ultimately, after providing so many workshops, I longed to be in one school or start a preschool. I partnered with the City of West Linn to offer a Mommy and Me program, which was a huge success, and we considered starting a preschool. But that fall when my son was mid-way through third grade, we realized the benefit of a Montessori education, so we enrolled him. The very next day, I was offered the job as an Assistant Guide.

This phase was my "pause" because it was a much slower pace than I had been used to, and the role leaned into what the students wanted to do. I worked with a Guide who inspired me to listen more and settle in. Rather than offering solutions, I learned to allow students to guide their way while I supported them. This shift opened me to so much more and helped shape my ability to lead summer camps at FMES and create broader courses and books like the one you are reading now.

Reading these stories, you can see that fun isn't just a nice addition—it's a bridge. It connects lessons from school to home, sparks new conversations, and even opens up parts of ourselves we might keep hidden. Showing up and being present allows us to take small, playful actions that ripple outward in big ways.

The reason I am sharing them with you is that you can integrate them into your conversations and lessons with others too.

If you are a teacher just add a colorful food each day to talk about, learn your numbers by counting healthy foods. Instead of giving candy treats, pass out inspirational quotes/coloring pages. Remember the Sad Soul© exercise from earlier? The banana relay, the laughter, and the creative challenges are all ways to open up that "sad soul" safely and joyfully. Each time you choose to engage, laugh, or try something playful—even in difficult moments—you are practicing how to show up fully. As we saw in the workshops, it's not about being perfect or winning first place; it's about participating, connecting, and allowing yourself to experience life in the moment.

The reflective takeaway is simple: small choices, when paired with fun, can transform experiences, relationships, and perspectives. Talk about what "healthy" means to others in conversations and be open to what unfolds.

Start small, notice the moments, and watch how playful actions can shift not just your day, but the lives around you.

Here are some ways to reframe challenges with fun:

Challenge: A project feels too big, and you want to give up
Fun is found in perspective. Break the project into small, doable steps and turn it into a game. If you're spreading gravel, focus on the sound of the rocks clattering into the wheelbarrow, the steps you're getting in, and the satisfaction of watching progress happen. Sweat can feel frustrating—or it can feel like a victory dance in motion.

Challenge: You spill bread dough all over the floor
Yes, it's a mess, but it's also a chance to make fun out of it. Crank up the music and dance while you clean. Turn the kitchen accident into an opportunity to clean. Then head to the store with

a playful mindset, and maybe grab something new (like olives!) to upgrade your recipe. Sometimes the "do-over" ends up better.

Challenge: Traffic is at a standstill
Instead of fuming, make it fun. Play your favorite playlist and turn the car into a mini concert hall. Try a language app, listen to a comedy podcast, or roll down the windows and people-watch. The time passes quicker when you see it as "bonus time" for joy.

Challenge: The kids are fighting again
Add fun by turning it into a silly game. Challenge them to argue in opera voices or using only pirate language. Laughter breaks the tension and shifts the energy for everyone. (And honestly, sometimes adults can benefit from this too!)

Challenge: Exercise feels like a chore
Find the fun by switching it up—dance in your living room, hula-hoop, try pickle ball with friends, or just walk somewhere new with a podcast you love. Movement doesn't have to feel heavy—it can feel like play.

Challenge: A friend talks behind your back
Instead of sinking into hurt or anger, add fun by addressing it directly in a playful way. You could say, "Well, if that rumor were true, then I'd probably do—what do you think?" By lightening the mood, you open space for honesty without making it tense. Co-create scenarios together that shift into laughter.

Challenge: Household chores pile up
Turn it into a challenge or game. Time yourself folding laundry, make it a family race, or put on a podcast while you scrub. Adding music is the easiest hack—suddenly a dance party!

Now It's Your Turn to Try...

Challenge: _____
Turn it into a challenge or game. _____
_____
_____

Challenge: _____
Turn it into a challenge or game. _____
_____
_____

Challenge: _____
Turn it into a challenge or game. _____
_____
_____

Notes...

Surprises Can be Fun!
Sometimes curiosity surprises you. One of my favorite examples is how we do road trips. We pick a destination—sometimes a city or a specific place to visit—but don't plan our stops, lodging, or daily activities ahead of time. Along the way, we prioritize parks and waterfalls or activities, yet leave room for the unexpected.

A couple of years ago my kids and I set out on a two week road trip to see friends who had moved to Dallas, Texas. Our trip started in Oregon and we drove to Crater Lake, then my daughter found a place to eat breakfast in Las Vegas so we headed that direction. On our way we were trading off driving and had enough energy that we kept going and going. At one point we stopped in the middle of nowhere in Nevada to enjoy the very dark sky and watch falling stars for an hour while we snacked on our dinner. The stars felt like they were right there and you could almost touch them. Our drive continued...

When I got tired, I found a good spot to stop and rest. My kids had said they wanted to go to Area 51, we woke up the next morning and that is where we were parked! We were the first in the gift store and got to watch the sun come up with those plastic aliens. In a couple of hours we were in Las Vegas and eating crapes for breakfast. Next, was the Hoover Dam. The temperature was HOT and I was looking forward to our one camping destination near a river to go kayaking. As it turned out there was a fire in the area and it was closed. I was about to turn around, yet my kids said we just needed to go get some ice cream and take a break. So that's what we did. Next thing I knew we were driving to Lake Havasu in Arizona. We met a family who gave us all kinds of ideas on places to go and stay in Arizona. Flagstaff and Sedona were the next day and then onto the Caves in New Mexico and the long, long drive to Dallas, Texas from there. After spending five days with them we had a wonderful Sunday showing up for the longhorn cattle drive in Fort Worth, Texas and then a memorable night where we ended up camping on a cattle farm. The next morning we woke up to baby steers and heifers all around us.

Moments like these remind me that life doesn't have to be rigid. Sometimes the best memories come from letting go of expectations and opening yourself to discovery.

Curiosity transforms ordinary days into adventures, and even small decisions—like which path to take or which sunset to pause for—become opportunities to engage fully and playfully with the world around you.

Be Patient and Present
Which reminds me of another moment when I was walking my dog and my daughter's puppy along a shallow river. I decided we'd do a creek walk, even though I don't have full feeling in the bottom of my leg. I've taught the dogs to walk slowly and give me support on a tight leash when I need it.

As we were in the middle of the river, water just passing our ankles, the dogs discovered a big branch. Watching them decide how to carry it back was hilarious—they went from sharing the branch, to tug-of-war, to dropping it, and then chasing after it again. I realized I just needed to stop, laugh, and enjoy the moment. And then something amazing happened: the branch seemed to point us to a new part of the river to explore. When we stay present, even small adventures can reveal something bigger.

When have you been in awe of what unfolded due to just going with the flow and seeing what unfolds?

Brainstorm or make a list of some things you would like change right now so that you can experience being present:

Our business coach often advised us to split our time throughout the week, month and year into different categories and I find this concept works well here too because I have been sharing ideas businesses and people use to get through a challenge.

So reflect below and figure out this challenge by looking at your broad range of job titles:

The Dreamer - the dreamer and inventor can show up daily and you could spend at least a day a week in these shoes coming up with ideas, drawing or writing

The Planner - the plans come from setting a goal and then setting specific times that tasks are completed in order to get to all of your goals. You could have a daily planner part for 1-2 hrs.

The Envisioner - this part of you envisions what they want: the big picture thinker may include what activities you are setting out to do this month, this season and this year - Maybe this part gets one to three days over the month and definitely one day each season to come up with what it is the next season you want

The Doer - this is the part of you that gets things done to keep the house or your system working well. This part is present a lot of your time as it thinks about the foods you are eating, water you are drinking throughout your day, when and where you walk and get fit, and the household chores that keep the house going.

Appreciating All The Ways that We Are
Moments like these remind me that life doesn't have to be rigid. Sometimes the best memories come from letting go of expectations and opening yourself to discovery. Curiosity transforms

ordinary days into adventures, and even small decisions—like which path to take or which sunset to pause for—become invitations to engage fully and playfully with the world around you. And when we practice leading with curiosity in the light moments, we build a kind of inner flexibility that helps us navigate the heavier ones.

Curiosity doesn't erase the hard parts of life, but it gives us a way to move through them with openness instead of shutting down. It reminds us that even in seasons of struggle, there is still room to notice beauty, ask questions, and discover what might be possible next.

How would you like to lean into a part of you or get more curious about how you live your life now?

Chapter 5

Love Yourself More

To get where you want to go, you need the ability to see both the big picture and the small details. First, imagine your future and what you truly want. Sometimes it might be totally clear, so then just imagine time with those you love or a sweet little vacation doing something you like. Then, shift your focus back to the present and take small, meaningful steps. By holding both visions—where you're going and where you are—you can move forward with clarity, purpose, and love for who you're becoming.

Even though I was doing what I understood I needed—eating healthy, staying active, resting—In 2018 I had recently undergone a major leg surgery after being hit head-on by a skier. After three weeks, I felt good enough to go to my daughters' track meet one evening, but perhaps is was too much or an infection was already stirring and I didn't even know it. That Friday when I went to PT, my therapist noticed something different and we removed the bandages to find a bad infection. We scheduled a visit with my doctor for Monday and over the weekend I got a high fever and had to stay in bed.

During that surgery, I had what I can only describe as a near-death experience. I found myself above the operating table, watching and listening as four doctors debated whether to amputate my leg. I heard a really strong message, "What about you?"

As I was in this in-between state, images flashed through my mind and I reflected on my life. I had lived a lot of my life with, "What If I do this, then that will happen". But instead of staying stuck in a reactive state of "What ifs," I made a decision to listen to "What is." I focused on what was true: I was active in my community, I was inspiring and encouraging others, I was coaching ski racing—which I loved—and I was raising healthy, independent children.

Then, I heard it again, louder and clearer: "What about you?" Instead of living for reactions, what if I started being proactive about living?

As the doctors were trying to make a decision on what to do. The voice said: "If you send LOVE to yourself and your leg, you will thrive. No longer will you have to wonder about 'What ifs.' You will begin to understand 'What is.'"

I woke up later in my hospital room—machines hooked up to me, a bed alarm on—and all I could do was focus on one thing: sending the word L-O-V-E to my leg and body.

That became my focus. Such a powerful lesson in such a short amount of time.

Living with intention is not just about the food we eat, the activities we do, or the job we pursue. It's all of that—but grounded in deep love for the one person living this life: you.

It was right in front of me, and yet I had forgotten to acknowledge myself. In order to heal, I had to love myself first. It sounds so simple. But we're surrounded by nay-sayers and distractions. You see, growing up, I learned differently and in business I was able to creatively solve problems.

Do you know how many times I had to stay in from recess just to write the word "the" over and over again? Or how many times I was teased for mispronouncing someone's name when I read it aloud? Just last week, while substitute teaching, I came across a student with a name that sounded nothing like how it was spelled. We worked together using phonetic word combinations so I could get it right. Thankfully, kids today are more understanding.

When Pressure Creates Diamonds

Because I was conditioned as a child as someone who was most likely going to do it differently or have someone say that I wans't doing it right, I attracted just that in my spouse. He was very good at pointing out my flaws—telling me my clothes didn't look right or that I was doing things wrong. Over time, I lived with a lot of second-guessing and began to feel that my choices were never good enough. A lot of that stress was secretyly hidden within me and sometimes I didn't even know if I should be alive.

It took a near-death experience to realize I wasn't supposed to die yet. And coming back to life with a new perspective made it clear: I needed to make some major life changes. When I started loving myself, I began to heal. I'm sharing this with you because I don't want you to have to die to learn the same lesson. Instead, let my experience empower your own.

Maybe your life has brought you to a place of frustration or despair. Maybe now is the time to say: Enough is enough.

When I started loving myself and leading with love toward myself in everything I did—even in all of my mistakes like saying the wrong words, spelling things wrong, waking up late, missing an appointment, being too early, or eating what others label as good or bad food—I began to realize how important it is to surround yourself with similarly loving people and experiences. I had to make some big, hard changes.

Listening to YOU

The voice continued: "You know exactly what YOU need to do. Be the example that anything is possible." Coming back to being in that hospital bed, where every 3-4 days I was having another surgery and they kept a wound vac on the open surgery site in hopes to get rid of the infection. Only issue was I had a lot of allergies to medicines that could kill the infection. My body was fighting against me and yet I had this one strong message that seemed to win this time. I was simply focused on sending love to my leg and to myself. There was no chatter, the negative self-talk was silent. I was fully present in the moment. I listened to recordings of my daughter playing the piano and kept the lights low. I talked to my son on the phone. Love, love, love.

I stayed very present, focused solely on loving to heal and healing to love. When I had the energy, I would do some watercolor painting in bed. But most of the time, I just lay there, focusing on sending intentional love. After all of that intense thinking, I set out not only to create a healing plan to help me live better, but also to research what would support healing with less stress and inflammation.

The next three weeks in the hospital were rough. I had allergic reactions to most of the antibiotics. I underwent six more surgeries. Each surgery was to clean out the infection and try to save my leg. Each surgery included going under and some of the surgeries even resulted in mini-strokes or troubles getting the trech in. They weren't easy and yet they were required in order for me to live. After each surgery, I returned to my hospital room with a wound vac over the open incision and a cord hanging down to release the infection. I couldn't walk. Only a wheelchair or use a walker and hop on one foot to the bathroom within the room. I didn't speak much. Noises and lights were too much and I just preferred to sleep or listen to quiet music. Visitors didn't come because they just wanted me to heal. And later I found out the only words I was really saying clearly was "No" so when someone asked to come visit, I guess I told them NO.

I was really weak—and yet I had a new joy within me, one that was brighter than ever. With limited words spoken, I couldn't really share all that I had learned, all that was now within. I was sad that I didn't have the strength to speak up and create the sentences that were within.

Once I was home, I had to give myself medicine ten hours a day through a PICC line, for ten weeks. It was one of the toughest situations I've ever faced. I had to drain my wound and take care of an open wound for ten months. I couldn't take normal showers or go out much. I still was expected to work part-time that summer because I had been the one who brought in most of our families income, so having me not work was not possible. I still was a mom to two great kids and I still wanted to be making meals for the family. I tried to make it to events like baseball games and allow the kids to have friends over, but everything was slower and took a lot more planning.

Challenges are Real
One time no one was able to get my son to his baseball game, and since I was finally approved to drive the car, I decided we could do this. My 10 year old son at the time helped get his gear and the wheelchair in. When we got to his game, we realized there was no parking up close for my car, so he would need to run over with all his gear by himself. It took a couple of trips, but he did it! I realized how we had all grown through the tough experience and how this resilience would help later in life. I was able to park and roll over in my wheelchair. As I sat back behind everyone, I realized the coach wouldn't let him play his favorite position because he was slightly late. My heart sunk.

When I came home, I shared the story with tears. My daughter made a card with this saying on it that helped me get through: ***"Sometimes the only way through is through."***

One day, I was in a parking lot by myself and as I was trying to get the wheelchair into the car, it rolled away. I had to jump on one foot across the parking lot to get it. In spite of what I'd heard from the doctors that I would never walk again, I decided I needed to also know how to get around on one leg. I set the wheelchair aside that night and figured out how to get up and down off the floor without using my injured leg. I practiced 50 times a day and often used hand crutches as well. Still, when I went out in public or left the house, I used the wheelchair—because I wasn't stable yet on uneven surfaces.

Your Support System
That summer, I continued my favorite job as a summer camp director—only this year since I wasn't as mobile I hired an assistant to help. My speech therapist and I worked on setting up plans in a notebook and resources in one spot so it was easier for our leaders to find what they were looking for. One incredible part was writing out scenarios of what to do if something happened and then on the back of the page, we had space to write out what we actually did in the situation. By breaking down all the tasks and information into do-able ways, I was able to stress less and enable my assistant to do more. .

My memory and finding words was different. I practiced new ways to memorize campers names. I repeated and rhymed. I wrote lists. We made back up plans to the back up plans. When I couldn't come up with the right words to say or mumble whatever I wanted to say. I used pictures on my phone and would point to those. Eventually I found out I had Aphasia—a speech language disability that affects ones ability to speak, but not their intelligence. It was very frustrating and I was so thankful for my speech therapist who helped and gave ideas on what I could do.

Out of everything, I realized Aphasia is one of the toughest hidden disabilities. It doesn't just affect what you say, it also affects some of what you learn and remember. It doesn't affect your intelligence, yet it does affect how people often read you.

Learning Through Healing

At the end of the summer, my speech therapist connected me to the Love Your Brain yoga (LoveYourBrain.org) program where I was able to take an in-person yoga class, even with aphasia, traumatic brain injury (TBI) and leg disability. In this class that was primarily on the floor and went slow due to others disabilities as well, I was able to see how I could use yoga, my breath work and mindset to heal. Over time, my yoga practices, having wonderful speech and physical therapists, I found a way—with love—to strengthen my leg and mindset.

Ten months after my first leg surgery and after seven surgeries done over ten weeks on that leg break... I walked.

In December I had one more surgery to remove the screws so that I could ski... I didn't coach ski racers that year in 2018/19, but I did get in ten half days and for spring break took my kids to Mt. Bachelor as that was what we were going to do the year before. When we went it was a gorgeous sunny day, so I decided to take them to the top and figured I could just go back and forth slowly and get myself down the hill. As the kids saw the shoot and really smooth run off they went! My plan to take it slow worked, yet my kids were not there. We stuck with our normal rule to go back to the last chair we were on. Sure enough, the kids were there hooping and hollering that I *finally* made it down. Finally!

The next season I was able to go back to ski race coaching and being with my kids on the mountain. Still, I tailored my days and selected trails that were smoother. I decided to coach just one day a week and work with younger athletes who didn't have to fly off of jumps or do the steeps. I knew I could pace myself for more days of fun in the future!

Healthy & Fun Choices for Me, too!

In addition to getting back to the mountain to ski, getting back in my car to be able to drive, and getting back so I could walk, I realized that for me to thrive beyond LOVING myself more, I could lean on the Healthy & Fun Choices™ educational program that I had been teaching others for years. This is what you are reading right now!

Going through all I went through, provided me so much insight into priorities and making sure to keep moving, to find new ways to do yoga, to find groups who could help me feel better about having Aphasia, to eat good food and to keep staying in activities like ski race coaching that I so much enjoyed. I also realized coming back to life that wanting to live has a lot to do with mindset and the people you surround yourself with. I knew that long term I needed to make some adjustments in where I live and who I live with, at the same time I was wanting to keep the family together if the relationship could grow along with what I had learned through my comeback.

Big Changes Challenge You or Create You

That spring, I lost my job as the summer camp director, we sold our house and downsized to 1/6th living space and we were forced indoors due to the pandemic!

I had just realized I wanted to be outside more and now this. I was still in physical therapy, speech therapy, vision therapy, neurofeedback and more. I had to get creative quick—I thought I can lead business leaders to do business online and I can teach teachers healthy and fun classes to persevere. So many things didn't make sense in my marriage and I had to trust that time would help me figure it out. I took one day at a time. Sometimes big challenges, create big opportunities!

Chapter 6

Honor Your Creativity

We all have creative brains. Your brain's main purpose is to protect you, but within it, we carry both logic and creativity. Sometimes it can be tricky to know which part to listen to, especially when ideas buzz around like a bee trapped in a mason jar.

After my leg injury and brain injuries, I realized just how important it is to slow down—to give my processing speed time to catch up with my creative brain. Communicating clearly took patience, practice, and a lot of retraining.

Creativity is the ability to generate ideas, thoughts, or processes—and often involves words. Taking an idea from your mind and turning it into something you can share isn't always simple. If your brain is busy or overwhelmed, you may feel distracted, notice too much at once, or even freeze. That's when anxiety can creep in, and tasks that once felt exciting may start to feel impossible.

Negative Self-Talk is Sneaky
I've learned that negative self-talk is one of the sneakiest traps for creative minds. My inner critic sometimes got so loud I started to believe it. There were moments when I even questioned whether I wanted to keep going. Finding Dr. Wayne Dyer's *Your Erroneous Zones* was a turning point. He taught me that pain isn't always a signal to panic—it can simply be a way of getting your attention.

Through self-help books, podcasts, and reflection, I've discovered strategies to reframe my thoughts and approach c challenges with curiosity rather than fear. One saying I developed is: SAME NERVE, DIFFERENT RESPONSE.

Think about hitting your funny bone—you might laugh, or even laugh so hard you cry. Pain and laughter travel along the same nerve; they're both trying to get your attention. Once I realized this, I could apply it more broadly. Pain, discomfort, or overwhelm doesn't have to stop creativity—it's just a signal. Responding differently allows your creative brain to thrive, even in the midst of challenges.

Honoring your creativity means noticing what your brain is telling you, pausing when needed, and giving yourself permission to respond in a way that nurtures growth, joy, and expression. ***You are you...You are enough.***

More Time to...
In 2010, while on vacation in Maui, Hawaii, I had some extra time to myself—my parents had taken the kids for the morning. I stepped out onto the lanai, leaned back, and fully noticed the sunshine, the birds singing, and the warm breeze. And then it hit me: we can choose the words we focus on. We also get to choose how we interpret the words we hear—and what stories or ideas they spark.

In just that moment as I sat there I experimented with my idea—when a worry or random thought popped into my mind—as they often do—I made the choice to focus on the word "sunshine." Immediately, I felt more connected to the sun's rays, basking in both the light and the word. I smiled.

I grabbed a notebook and began writing about this idea, testing it in my own life. I've always needed to experiment before sharing something with others. Back when we ran a graphic design business, I tested everything—printers, mailing processes, social media trends, writers—before creating logos or campaigns for clients. Listening to and experimenting with words felt just as important.

The next morning, while having breakfast outside, I looked to my left—and there sat one of my favorite educators and speakers, Dr. Wayne W. Dyer. I realized he was giving a workshop that day at the hotel. What were the chances?

When his table was waiting for food, I decided to be bold and introduce myself. I told him how his book, Your Erroneous Zones and many other books, had helped me overcome the pain of endometriosis by refocusing my energy, and how I had become more present with my family through mindful choices. Then I asked if tickets were still available for his talk.

He smiled and asked, "Why did you come to Hawaii?" I said, "To spend more time with family." He replied, "Then keep doing that. I'll personally record the workshop for you tonight. I'm also in the States in a few months—you can come to my show then." I was ecstatic. It felt magical to meet him, and I realized something powerful: when you focus on the good, more good shows up. So take my word for it—play with this concept: when a negative thought pops up, replace it with a word that inspires good thoughts or memories. Shift your focus and see what happens next.

For example, when I feel overwhelmed by frustrating stories in my head, I shift to the word sunshine or joy or laughter. Instantly, I'm reminded of sunny days at the beach, finding heart-shaped rocks, and hearing my daughter's laughter in my mind. With one word, the stories in my mind become lighter, brighter, and more connected. I did come out with a book with this idea in it, and the information was great and the journal challenging our thoughts but I felt like I needed a book that spoke more into The Healthy & Fun Choices Way. So if you want the words, message me and I'll give you that book too or send you a link where you can get it for a special.

Adjusting Your Sails

Adjusting your direction doesn't mean you're giving up. It might mean you need to learn something new, overcome a challenge, or gain a story worth sharing later. If adjusting feels frustrating, step back. Reconnect with your why, or pick a word that fills you with positive energy and let it go.

Your creative brain is a directional system—pulling you toward what you want and who you're meant to become. Your dreams, your challenges, and your ability to ask questions are all part of this process, guiding you to discover more about yourself.

Peter Senge calls this Creative Tension—like a rubber band stretched between your hands. When the tension is just right, you feel it—you're learning and moving forward. Too little, and the rubber band slips away. Too much, and it breaks. Finding your balance is where growth happens.

If you have a rubber band or hair tie nearby, play with this concept. Stretch it just enough—what happens when it holds? Stretch it too far or too little—what breaks or slips?

How can the concept of Creative Tension help you honor your creativity and explore your thoughts, words, and actions? Notice, experiment, and see what emerges.

Creativity isn't just about making art or writing—it's how your brain experiments, explores, and guides you toward what matters most. It's in the way you notice, imagine, and respond to life's challenges and joys. Honoring your creativity means giving yourself space to play, make mistakes, shift your focus, and embrace new ideas without judgment.

Remember: your creative brain is always working—even when it feels messy or overwhelming. By practicing curiosity, experimenting with words or thoughts, and paying attention to what your mind and body are telling you—turn overwhelm into insight, anxiety into action, and ideas into something meaningful.

Honor Your Creativity

Here is a good spot to just take a pause.

Breathe and notice your inhale and exhale.
    Adjust your shoulders down and back and
        lead with your heart.
Breathe again...

Take a moment and ask yourself:

What three choices could I make today that will help me?

When my mind feels stretched or stuck, how can I shift my perspective to move forward with curiosity or that Creative Tension instead of fear?

Your creativity is yours to nurture. Protect it, experiment with it, and celebrate, it will guide you in ways you can't always anticipate, and it will continue to show you the magic that's already within you.

Here's your space to doodle, draw or reflect...

A doodle...

Chapter 7

Reframe It

Another way to work through challenges is to "Reframe It." My business coach, Dr. Thomas Jones, taught this in his renewal course—sometimes it's not what we're seeing that helps us, but how we see it. David McNally's book Even Eagles Need a Push shares a similar idea. His chapter on renewal reminds us that a new perspective creates momentum for moving forward.

Our first interpretation of an experience might not be true or wise. It could be your cautious brain trying to hold you back, while your creative brain knows there's a better way.

You can do this with anything you say or think:

I talked too much.
→ Reframe it: I had creative ideas to share.

Other people are more successful—look at their house and boat.
→ Reframe it: A big house and boat take a lot of time to maintain—now I see that I have more time.

My pain holds me back from eating out.
→ Reframe it: I'm able to cook foods that support me.

That friend on social media is living the best life!
→ Reframe it: She might not be sharing everything, look at what is good in my life and be happy with that!
Now it's your turn:

State an idea: _____
→ Reframe it: _____

State an idea: _____
→ Reframe it: _____

State an idea: _____
→ Reframe it: _____

State an idea: _____
→ Reframe it: _____

You can also do this with a therapist or a friend. Remember that sometimes the people closest to you may not want to hear about your inner critic or your struggles.

Sometimes, even with reframing, the real breakthrough isn't finding an "opposite" thought—it's simply finding a softer, lighter version. That small shift makes all the difference.

In my case, many of my close friends just wanted to fix me. For years, I was seen as broken, too sensitive, full of ideas, not following through, speaking harshly to myself—even though I looked put together on the outside, I felt terrible inside.

So when I shared concerns, many didn't want to hear it and sharing made me feel worse. But as I came back to life after all my accidents and surgeries, I realized something: Being fixed was the last thing I needed. What I was craving was loving support even someone to just be with me and witness the hard and offer support or a hand with my leg, traumatic brain injury and aphasia. Now that I know so much about TBI and Aphasia, I wish my family took those classes and went to support groups.

What I really needed was love. Just love—for who I truly was and who I was becoming.

Learning to love myself wasn't easy—it meant making some of the most painful choices of my life.

The hardest part of learning how to love myself was recognizing that I had let go of people in my life who made me feel like I wasn't enough. I had to make some incredibly difficult choices: ending a 25-year marriage and saying goodbye to a friend who had once meant everything to me since I was seven years old.

In both cases, there were too many areas where we just didn't align. They couldn't support me as "the new me." Even with all of my disabilities and new thinking around being okay, they still judged, compared, and made me feel like I was in trouble for every little thing and that I always needed to come to meet them or do whatever they needed, even in front of my own needs. But here's what I know now...some of the hardest choices lead to a lot of tears and a new reality that includes less stress, more joy. You have this one life—give it your all.

Counseling & Support Groups Help You Talk Through
By finding a counselor who helped me understand my Internal Family Support (IFS) and talk through what I experience an how different parts of me feel and acknowledge reactions, I was able to learn how to witness and grow. Additionally, I found the Aphasia Recovery Connection group, Love Your Brain yoga and mindset classes and retreats, and was able to make friends with people who share similar challenges. My internal systems and self-talk began to improve so much!Connecting with others that are going through similar life experiences allow you to feel more blessed and happy!

My Aphasia Ambassador Community Group has three others who have been through so much and still they are getting out and talking to groups, putting on workshops, leading conferences and sharing more about Aphasia and why it is important for people, doctors and nurses to know how they can support us.

We're here for more than just keeping the human race going. Maybe learning to love yourself and take action from that place is enough. For me, it's that—and more.

I was able to lean in to my mistakes. To heal and realize the mistakes I was making were actually magical. What I mean by this is that when I'm feeling "less than" or like I didn't do enough, I am able to look at nature and see how mistakes and change lead to growth. Thankfully as well, my kids allow me to laugh and smile and recognize that we are all in this together.

And sometimes, life sends reminders that we are enough exactly as we are—in the most unexpected ways.

One day last year, after a rough weekend, I went to my favorite park and sat on a bench to soak in the sun. I heard birds chirping—hummingbirds darting and dancing all around me. They seemed to be having a party, as if trying to tell me something important.

I looked to my right—and there, sitting on the red bench right next to me was a small ceramic heart. Carved into the design, it said: "You Are Enough."

If that's not a sign, I don't know what is. I decided that it was for me and I put it in my pocket. As I left the park, the attendant asked if I had found any little pieces of artwork as an artist had specifically left treasures for people to pick up and enjoy.

I showed the heart and we all smiled.

So, what signs have you found on your walk through life?

What do you feel you need to know right now?
What's your "aha" moment—that moment when you finally believe: "Yes, I am enough."? I hope so! Reach out to me if you need more resources or a conversation, I am here for you.

Grateful for Friends Who Give Perspective & Grace
I am grateful for the friends and teachers who, through numerous experiences, helped me discover a different approach to challenges. My oboe teacher, Bob Scott had many challenges to overcome. During World War II, he reached down to help a fallen friend, and a grenade exploded right in front of him, severing all of his fingers and killing his friend. Not one to give up, he returned home to his wonderful wife, and eventually, going back to playing and teaching the oboe.

Even with his disabilities, he figured out how to keep playing—and to inspire others to do the same. I'm forever grateful for how he encouraged me to keep going, even if I hadn't practiced enough, missed a note, squeaked, or thought I couldn't do it all. He helped me discover that I could. "Mistakes," he said, "are the beauty—each their own unique way of making music."

I'm also grateful for my ex-husband and that we had the courage to split up and get a divorce. We spent 33 years together, and while we didn't always see eye to eye, our time together taught me lessons about standing up for oneself, knowing when something is good and to trust your intuition, and how to politely say no and set boundaries. Often we approached challenges differently, and there were moments when humor lightened difficult situations. We also were in business together for many years, sometimes we worked really well together and other times we didn't agree. We were both graphic designers, so you can see how this could be hard when we were needing to create excellent work on deadlines, trying to create and simplify messages that were sometimes hard to understand and also keep the cash flow and client work positive. Add having children, which were truly my favorite experience in this life time on top of busy schedules. We learned how to prioritize and chunk time, both for ourselves, our work, and our family. Through it all, I learned how essential time and mindset are to our well-being, and those lessons ultimately shaped The Healthy & Fun Choices® Way. I also discovered how often we try to look "fine" on the outside while carrying something very different inside—and that true ease comes when our inner and outer lives align, supported by people who value our real selves.

Aligning Internal Dialogue
In addition to relationships being aligned on the inside and outside, I also want my inner self-talk to match the peace and positivity I strive to show on the outside. I want who I am privately and publicly to reflect the same sense of calm, kindness, and authenticity. That's when, I believe, we're truly living.

It amazes me how many lessons life offers, and how we get to choose which ones we want to cherish and learn from. This book is about choice—about helping yourself discover what truly matters to you. It's like taking a magnifier on parts of your life and realizing that you get to discover how you want to see it. The more good you focus on the more good appears. When you are going through tough or challenging times, or notice fears and worries popping in more than normal, you get to think about your responses and how much time you put into being with whatever it is and how it aligns with your overall vision of yourself and how you want to be perceived as well.

In the last year, I had an opportunity to be more involved in the Aphasia community. Being selected to be part of a mentor or support group allowed me to be connected to others who also have aphasia and are creating more awareness about what aphasia is and how it affects us, but not our intelligence. Each week we would meet and often the meetings went different than what I expected. I had to learn how to adjust and be open to what was next because I felt like my internal dialogue includes so much conversation around aphasia and so perhaps I should be communicating this more with others externally. This is a challenge and it brings up emotions and uneasiness of being vulnerable. Through the process I have learned a lot about myself and that I can help others communicate better since I am a writer and graphic designer. I realized how I can understand others even when they cannot find their words and that my intuition of listening and asking questions typically leads to greater understanding.

What I've realized is that if we don't choose—if you don't act on your ideas—someone else will. How do I know this? I gave my ideas away to numerous speakers, business owners, and others, and got to sit back and watch their success! I remember putting a lot of time and energy into a blog on my website only to find our someone I knew who was in a different business was copying my blog and using it for their own. At first, I was a bit upset. Then, my mom said it was a compliment, which is true. Yet, it made me feel like they had taken something from me without first asking my permission, so that felt invalidating. I had to choose if I wanted them to keep doing that, if I wanted to keep investing my time into others benefits, or if I instead wanted to start compiling my ideas and eventually write books. I chose the later. It has taken me many years to gather everything together to get to this point of what you are reading, right now. Maybe that's exciting. Maybe it's frustrating. It's taken me too many years to get this done—but here you are, reading it. My hope is that something in these stories will spark something in you.

Gaining Perspective From Random Opportunities
One of my favorite summers in college was when I won a graphic design internship. I started with small jobs that sometimes turned into bigger projects. I learned to see what each situation could teach me. I'll never forget when I was asked to design an invitation and poster for a new concert series at the zoo. They said it would feature a jazz artist.

When the artist called, he asked to speak directly to the designer, so they connected him to me. On the phone, he had a low voice with a strong southern accent. I had no idea who it would be. Then he said his name—and I jumped out of my seat: "B.B. King!?!" Having played the oboe and loved music, I really liked his work—he was the king of blues! He had this way of playing that just captivated the audience and pulled you in with complete curiosity. Music has inspired me to listen more to all the sounds, the beats and the pauses.

He laughed and confirmed it was him. He even offered me front-row tickets to his concert. I was so excited! My excitement even inspired the rest of the studio. The older designers decided that I shouldn't really work on this project alone now that it was revealed who I would be designing the invitation and posters for the Zoo Concert. Even then, I learned I had to stand up for myself and not just let others take it away because of my excitement. This moment made me realize how being open to opportunities—even ones that seemed small at first—can lead to unforgettable experiences.

Another time working at that same job as an intern graphic designer, a photographer in the same building needed help with a photo shoot. He came down to our studio near Saturday Market in downtown Portland. We were in an older building that had really creaky floors and high ceilings. The walls showed their age with the streaking on the wood and bricks showing through.

I thought oh I bet the photographer is wanting to feature the details of the space in his photo shoot. The other designers were too busy, so they sent me.

As I walked into his studio I realized it wasn't a photo shoot featuring the building, rather he had some props set up and a big tall 14 ft. ladder positioned off to one side. I asked him, "How can I help?" As I walked in, I looked over and saw a very tall basketball player. The photographer said he was having troubles getting an image of him that could fit in his photo frame and asked me to help him figure out the best angle. I asked if I could go up the ladder.

Once up high, I found the perfect shot and said, "If you get up here and have him stretch his arms out wide in opposite directions while he holds a basket ball, you'll probably get a pretty cool shot." So I held the ladder and motioned to the very tall athlete to stretch wide, hold his chin up a bit and bring his shoulders down and back so the shadows were just so. I was about 5'5" in height, very small in comparison and yet I felt like I could see all the details that would highlight him. I was not big into watching basketball as it was during ski season, so when the games were happening we were usually getting ready for the next day of skiing. As I left the photographers studio I realized I needed to look up who that was and what team he played for. I didn't say anything to the other designers, just said that the photo shoot went good and that it was just of a tall person.

A couple weeks later the photographer came into our studio with the tall athlete. The secretary was having a screaming attack by the time she could bring me up as they had a gift for me. They had brought in the results of the poster and wanted to personally sign the poster and thank me for the art direction that I offered. The tall athlete was none other than Shaquille O'Neal! I got a signed poster of him holding the basket ball out to the side with his arms stretched wide. This was 1993 and Nike went on to also have Jordan do the same pose, as you can imagine these posters became legendary iconic posters.

Being a graphic designer meant living in the moment—staying open to whatever came next. Whether arranging color palettes or running last minute to deliver a presentation, I learned to adapt and stay ready. That perspective that you gain from random experiences is priceless because you gain further understanding on how people react or how welcoming they are.

How Owning a Small Business Helped Navigate Change
When we started our own agency in 1994, I was young and many people thought we were too young. Yet, we did excel—taking on big, exciting projects. Then, we lost a huge client. Fortunately, we found the Small Business Marketing and Management class in an SBDC taught by Dr. Thomas Jones and it turned out to be just what we needed. Learning alongside other insightful business owners and working with them to grow their businesses was incredibly fulfilling for fifteen years!

We learned about doing business differently. I had always thought to be successful we needed to be located downtown. But since I was creative at night, a downtown setting wasn't a smart choice. Dr. Thomas Jones advised us about how we could work from home in 1996. At that time it wasn't normal. So we got ourselves a PO Box and met clients at coffee shops, restaurants and their offices for meetings.

Our business grew and we were able to dedicate Fridays to Go Kart racing, water skiing or hiking. Sometimes we could escape to our family cabin in central Oregon for a three day weekend. Instead of waiting to play when we retired, we integrated play into our every day schedules.

Our meetings and weekly schedules allowed for daytime walks at parks so we weren't so overwhelmed because presentations can be intense. In the evenings we made sure we were getting our exercise, doing yoga, playing soccer or futsal, or Aikido and hanging out with family to balance our creativity and solving big problems for clients.

We even adjusted our schedules depending on when we did what kind of work most effectively and efficiently. I was very creative at night when there were no distractions, so I often stayed up to 3 or 4am and met with my programmer when he was just starting his day. Then as I slept, he was able to work without distractions and we would meet mid-morning to go over website and app designs. There is no one way to work, there are a lot of different ways when you can reframe it for what works for you.

Having the ability to adjust our schedules with the ebb and flow of our work also allowed us to build our dream house with a gorgeous mountain view and coach ski racing in the winters.

When we added children to our family, we brought them with us to meetings and had activities they could do while we worked. Luckily my parents were next door and they could help support us, too. It was really special time that my children had being raised that way.

Being a female business owner for over three decades has allowed me to realize that life and business are continuously changing: that is a fact. I am proud that I have been able to put my kids first and have been able to adjust my career and time so that I could volunteer in their schools, coach sports and take breaks when needed. Soon our studio was located upstairs of our house and with a separate entrance. When our industry shifted to laptops and apps and we didn't need such a big space, we were able to turn the office into an AirBnB.

Phone usage in young kids have deterred activity books a bit, but my hope is as this book reaches more and more people, the activity books will too! You can help by sharing the books with others and putting the activity books in schools or as stocking stuffers at Christmas time!

Reframing It Even with Pandemic and Divorce
After recovering from my accidents, I came to understand just how vital The Healthy & Fun Choices Way has been to our family's resilience through some of the hardest times. During the pandemic, our home no longer felt like a safe space. It wasn't easy.

The kids and I moved into a house close to the farm where my daughter worked and the kids' schools. We created a new version of family. Their dad remains involved in their lives, and they make time to be together. We've learned to set clear boundaries and respect them—making things more balanced for everyone. Raising teens independently has given me the space to focus on my recovery with less stress and more joy.

Without the constant pressure of criticism, I'm more punctual, more organized, and no longer second-guess my decisions or worry as much about being judged. This new chapter has been a gift of clarity and self-care.

Still to this day we prioritize fitness and strength training, walks with dogs, yoga and rest, research on food prepping and making colorful meals at home, and my kids and I prioritize getting outdoors with friends.

Has there been any big changes that you have had in your life that allowed you to discover more from a different perspective?

Chapter 8

Mistakes are Magic

Writing has been a lifeline for me. After developing aphasia, writing became even harder—my typing was full of spelling errors because my brain struggled to find the right letters. Recording my words was tough, too, since I couldn't always find my words or form sentences correctly. Sometimes Siri couldn't even tell what I was saying.

Aphasia is a language processing disability that affects our ability to find words, speak up, speak clearly and often understand language as well. It does not affect our intelligence and is a difficult hidden disability. At the same time, I have met some of the most incredible and determined people to live a happy life!

How Technology, Counselors & Yoga Help Disabilities
Thank goodness for editors and being able to lean on my trained ChatGPT artificial intelligence friend who can help me when I can't find the right word, spell it or make sense of what I want to say. Since getting my Traumatic Brain Injury and Aphasia my typing has also been affected. I misspell almost every word I type in and a second later recognize the misspelling and fix it. What I do is speak or text into a note—which helps reduce my stress and allows me to find a variety of ways to communicate..

With Aphasia it affects our ability to speak and sometimes even speak up. I often say words without pronouncing all syllables or I mix up the order of how you are to say it. When I am stressed it is worse than when I can just go with the flow. Sometimes we do not complete sentences or might mumble. The hard part is we have to be okay with not speaking fully or correctly. For a long time I isolated myself and would do a lot of texting or communications over Facebook, but that didn't help me socially as I often found myself feeling "less-than."

Aphasia is for life, we can get better yet never fully retrieve it all as the damage in the brain in permanent. In my brain it is the frontal lobe and my hippocampus. I have what is called Weineker's or Receptive Aphasia. People with other kinds of Aphasia or Apraxia may not be able to speak at all or their language is altered.

Being in aphasia groups and becoming good friends with others, I have learned so many different ways to communicate and been inspired to help others communicate with slides, posters, and opening up my zoom for conversations that we can record and share with others. Right now Aphasia is not well known and one of my goals as an Ambassador is to help everyone know more about it. By getting the words out, we can further awareness and make it easier for nurses, doctors, teachers and care givers to know how they can help.

Sometimes I mumble, don't make sense at all or say "he" for "she" or "delete" for "down" some of the words are funny and we can laugh. But what about when I can't find the word or even describe it in the right way? I literally just have to skip it and move on.

Finding a good therapist helped me navigate life's hard moments and big changes. My counselor helps to reveal the habits and thoughts that shape my growth. I have found, what matters most is taking steady steps in conversations of what helps today. Bringing this book altogether has been a whole learning curve. Sometimes I am so worried about whether or not a story will come across right or if there will simply be typos. Maybe there's a book inside you waiting to be written, with support from a coach or mentor. If not now, when?

Unique Mistakes like Writing Backwards

I can type and read backwards, better than forwards. I was tempted to include a whole page, but my editor wisely said most people wouldn't get it. If this book ever frustrates you, remember it's your copy—you can write in it, fix it, or even pass it on.

Here is one sentence just for the fun of it! Why not?

LUFITUAEB ERA UOY - If you cannot read it, hold it up to a mirror and see what you see, and smile because it is true!

So, you might find mistakes in this book. As a copywriter, I used to have to work with an editor for 20 hours a week! That was hard. I love the fact now that our editors can just make the corrections needed right here in the copy.

We Crave Warmth

Beyond our ability to write or communicate, what about mistakes when we reach for something we know we shouldn't be eating? I still catch myself reaching for mochas, chocolate, popcorn, or chips as a reward or distraction. Right now a lot of people sit and do social media, play video games, scroll through reels or tiktok and they eat. Maybe you do it, too. Are you able to catch yourself and not just sit and eat while you play or scroll? What if you could try to pause, maybe grab some yoga poses, do some sit ups or push ups, take your dog for a walk or turn up the music and dance?

The stories we tell ourselves and others shape our lives—sometimes in surprising ways. One lazy Saturday, my family and I went to a local café in pajamas. Later, when my daughter wanted to see Santa, I told her the line was too long and we wouldn't get in. It wasn't true—I just didn't want to stand in line in pajamas. I regretted the little lie almost immediately, frustrated with myself. We went home and my son took a nap as my daughter and I started working on a puzzle. When he awoke and asked if we could go now, my daughter started telling a new story of why we couldn't go—also not true. I was astonished.

That moment showed me how powerful stories can be. They can hold us back or create false realities. Have you ever told a lie to steer a choice? Felt guilty afterward? I realized how important it is to watch what I think, say, and do—and how exciting life gets when we choose honesty.

Peter Drucker said, "The best way to predict the future is to create it." Our mistakes, big and small, are magic—opportunities to learn and grow.

Our words, ideas, conversations, and thoughts affect our health just as much as what we eat or how we move. Even dental health matters—it's where food first gets absorbed by your body.

Awareness begins with deciding how you want to think, feel, and live. That Santa story helped me see how even small white lies shift reality—and how many of us were taught to persuade through convincing stories. But honesty and effective communication can be far more powerful.

We've been trained to be critical—of ourselves and others—in school, sports, and family. To meet expectations, some exaggerate, lie, or assume. Even small fibs can lead to wasted time, guilt, anxiety, and low self-esteem. These feelings limit potential and contribute to physical and mental health struggles.

But you can choose your thoughts, words, and actions to benefit yourself and those around you. Living intentionally inspires others. From that moment of the Santa day, I made a promise to myself to be as honest and truthful as I can and what I notice is my kids and I have a lot less worry, fears and anxieties because we don't have to keep track of stories that aren't true and we can live more in the moment. Here's what I found is helpful... First, listen to your communication patterns and self-talk—the silent dialogue inside your head when you decide how to respond.

Do you struggle with stress, cravings, fatigue, or pain? Your body might be signaling it's time for change.

Change Takes Courage
It means filtering out distractions, standing up for yourself, and sometimes distancing from negativity. It may mean turning off the news, ignoring toxic comments, and letting go of worries beyond your control.

Did you know news often focuses on violence and problems to keep you watching? That cycle benefits advertisers, not you. You don't need to live in constant worry—try limiting your news intake and filling your screen with positivity. Or set a timer. Or if that's what you like, then just enjoy it. There may be seasons of wanting to watch more and others times not so much.

Notice how you tell stories or text—are you adding drama or just passing time? Try shifting your focus with a word like "love" or "sunshine" when negativity creeps in.

Your Time is Precious
You only have so much time each day and lifetime. Use it wisely. I regret sleeping much of my high school years away when I could have been learning skills, hanging out with friends, practicing sports or making money.

Let go of "coulda, woulda, shoulda" stories—they keep you stuck. You only have so much time each day—and in your lifetime. Use it wisely.

Instead of dwelling on regrets, choose a life you love by:
• Replacing negative self-talk with uplifting words.
• Setting limits on phone time.

- Changing your default browser or apps to something positive.
- Catching yourself when telling exaggerated stories.
- Offering compliments instead of criticisms.

Mistakes are inevitable but don't have to define you. Embrace them, learn from them, and keep moving forward. Take a moment: write down a mistake you've made, what you learned from it, and what you're grateful for.

Here's an idea: You could start a Gratitude Journal writing out 1-3 ideas you are grateful for! .
I am grateful for who I am because...

I am grateful for this person because....

I am grateful for where I live because...

Thoughts in time are not fixed. It moves with us, stretches around us, and reshapes itself with every season of our lives. When we grow, our ideas grows. When we are overwhelmed, time for our thoughts can feel more frustrating. When we are present, time and our thoughts soften. When resiliency takes root—when we begin finding our way back to ourselves—time begins to open again.

After difficult seasons, whether from illness, financial strain, parenthood, transitions, or emotional exhaustion, our relationship with time often changes. We don't return to time the way we once knew it. We rebuild it. We listen differently. We prioritize differently. **We hold our minutes with a little more care, because we've learned that time is not something we manage—it's something we honor.**

Chapter 9

Resiliency for Braver Living

L et's talk honestly for a moment—just you and me.

Resiliency sounds like a big, serious word, but it rarely begins in big or serious moments. It starts quietly, in the tiny choices you make on an ordinary day. It lives in the way you breathe when something hurts… the way you soften when you want to harden… the way you speak up when your words feel tangled… the way you keep going even when you'd rather hide.

If the last chapter reminded us that mistakes are magic, this one reminds us that resiliency is the art of trying again with a braver heart.

Resiliency isn't a trait some people are born with and others are not. It's a practice. A muscle. A way of being. And most importantly—it's something you can grow, shape, nurture, and return to whenever you need it.

It's part of The Healthy & Fun Choices Way because it makes everything else in your life possible. Without resiliency, choices feel overwhelming. With resiliency, they feel like invitations. So let's explore how resiliency actually shows up in your life—and how you can live braver from here forward.

Resiliency Begins in the Smallest Moments

Most people think resiliency is the ability to bounce back after something massive—an injury, a loss, a financial collapse, a breakup, a diagnosis. But the truth is, resiliency starts long before any of those moments happen.

Resiliency begins in the tiny places where you choose curiosity over hiding. It shows up when you try something new even though you feel unsure. It shows up when you speak even though your voice shakes. It shows up when you decide, "Okay... I'll try again."

For many of us—especially those living with aphasia, brain injuries, chronic pain, grief, or any kind of invisible challenge—resiliency is not about getting it perfect. It's about finding a way. Any way. Your way.

In the aphasia community, we practice this constantly. We learn to speak up even when we know words may come out mixed or sideways. We sing to strengthen the breath and rhythm of language. We interview each other on Zoom because conversation (even messy conversation) keeps connection alive. We hold up notes, or screens, or photos on our phones to help bridge meaning. We plan ahead. We practice. We laugh. And the beautiful thing? We understand each other. This is resiliency. This is community.

This is braver living.

Doing Things Differently IS the Bravery
One of the biggest misunderstandings about resiliency is the belief that "the right way" is the bravest way. But what if the bravest way is your way?

I teach yoga, and I often say the wrong word or mix up a cue. My tongue might choose a word that wasn't the one my brain intended, but the students figure it out. I don't need to apologize every time. They understand the meaning beneath the words.

And leaning on the wall? That's not cheating. That's being wise. Some days your balance is different. Some days your brain fires differently. Some days your body says, "Let's go slowly today," and that is still yoga. That is still presence. That is still strength.

There is no "one right way."
Not in yoga.
Not in communication.
Not in healing.
Not in life.

If you've ever seen someone with one arm tie their shoe, or someone blind navigate a hallway with perfect grace, or someone missing a limb climb a rock wall, you already know this: There are countless ways to live a full, beautiful life.
So why do we judge ourselves so harshly for being different? Resiliency is trusting that YOUR way—creative, adaptive, imperfect, honest—is exactly the right way for you.

Resiliency Is Speaking Up Even When It's Hard
I've had moments—many of them—when the words I wanted didn't come. When I paused midsentence. When I forgot the right name. When my brain stalled like a car on a cold morning. These moments used to embarrass me. They used to make me withdraw. They used to make me feel "less than."

But resiliency taught me something powerful: You can speak bravely even when you don't speak perfectly. Communication isn't about correctness—it's about connection. Resiliency is choosing connection over correctness, every time.

Pain Can Come Along for the Ride
Let's talk about pain—not to magnify it, but to acknowledge it. Pain is stubborn. It doesn't always wait until you're done doing life. It doesn't always stay quiet while you breathe, stretch, work, or move. That's the part no one likes to admit. But pain

doesn't have to be the enemy. It can be a companion you learn to travel with. Sometimes the bravest thing you can say is, "Okay pain, come with me. But you're not steering today."

Maybe you're walking a little slower, holding the railing, and breathing deeper. Maybe you're focusing on the view instead of the ache.

Maybe you're letting movement soften the pain rather than fighting it. Resiliency is not waiting for pain to disappear before you live. It's learning how to live—and even thrive—in partnership with the body you have today. *Your connecting to your cues and choosing to take action.*

Creativity Is a Form of Resiliency
Sometimes life asks you to reinvent yourself. Not because you failed, but because circumstances shifted underneath your feet. Financial changes. A new diagnosis. Losing someone you love. A sudden curveball. An unexpected job change.

In those moments, resiliency shows up in creativity. Not "bounce back," but "bend differently." Not "start over," but "start from here." Not "figure it out alone," but "reach out and collaborate." During times when my business changed drastically, it wasn't about "losing everything." It was about reinventing. Rewriting. Reimagining what my skills could become in a new chapter of life. Creativity, connection and community saved me. And, resiliency guided the way forward.

You don't need to have all the answers to take the next step. You just need to stay open to creative solutions.

Grief, Loss, and the Quiet Courage of Continuing
Let's acknowledge something important: resiliency isn't only built through challenges you overcome. Sometimes it's built through losses you learn to live with. There was a summer when

I lost two people who were essential to my life—one a longtime mentor and coach who understood me deeply, and one a lifelong friend who brought joy everywhere she went. Losing them felt like losing parts of myself. Resiliency didn't mean "moving on." It meant carrying their love forward, remembering their lessons. It meant allowing grief to soften rather than consume. It meant believing that I could keep going even when my heart felt heavy.

Resiliency is the quiet courage to continue loving, living, and showing up—even after life changes you.

Let's redefine bravery:
Bravery isn't loud, flawless or polished. Bravery is sitting in a room with people you love and saying, "I don't know how to explain this, but I'm going to try." Bravery is adjusting the yoga pose instead of pushing past your body's limits. Bravery is asking for help. Bravery is sharing what is on your mind with someone you love when you are just feeling down. Bravery is choosing joy in a moment that could lean toward despair. Bravery is saying, "I can't yet... but I'm still here." Bravery is trying even when the outcome is uncertain.

Resiliency and bravery go hand in hand: Resiliency helps you keep going. Bravery helps you speak, listen, adapt, and rise.

Bringing The Healthy & Fun Choices Way into Your Life
Here's the truth: You don't practice Healthy & Fun Choices by adding things to your life. You practice it by shifting the way you live the life you're already in.

Healthy & Fun Choices is a lens, a rythm or an awareness. A way of being. It means choosing presence over pressure. Trying instead of hiding. Curiosity instead of shame. Movement instead of stagnation. Creativity instead of self-criticism. Honesty instead of silence.

Play instead of fear. Connection instead of perfection.

It means letting your day soften instead of harden. With this way of being braver, you can pick what you love, even simple choices like color, breath, nature, and nourishment. You feel empowered to speak up and embrace the idea that your body, brain, and spirit are allowed to guide you. You can live this way in tiny doses, woven through your day, even in simple ways like a breath, pause, question, small choice, intention or a moment of kindness toward yourself.

Resiliency helps you make Healthy & Fun Choices the way you are—not an event, not a task, but a rhythm your life settles into. This prepares you beautifully for what comes next: redefining what "healthy" means for you.

Reflection Questions
Let these sit gently with you:

What does braver living look like for you today—
not someday, but now?

Where in your life could you practice a softer, more adaptable kind of resiliency?

What small choice could you make that would bring more Healthy & Fun energy into your day?

How might you speak up, try differently, or live more fully—
without waiting to be perfect?

*Because whether you're running a business,
a household, or your own personal comeback story—
the way you live each day matters.*

Chapter 10

Redefine Healthy

Many people believe that a successful life is measured by how much we accomplish, win, or earn—and that health is simply about what we eat or how often we exercise. But health is far more layered than that. As you've seen throughout this book, self-love and caring for our bodies allow us to show up more fully in relationships, in work, and in life. We also share a responsibility to broaden the conversation about what "whole health" truly means.

For those who teach, design, or inspire others, it becomes even more important to communicate the full picture—colorful foods, varied movement, mindfulness, creativity, and joy. Charts like the USDA food plate may have been a starting point, but they don't account for allergies, sensitivities, or the wide range of lifestyles people live. No single model fits all. Health must be inclusive, adaptable, and personal.

Redefining healthy starts with awareness—understanding your body's needs, signals, and rhythms. When you begin noticing how food, movement, and mindset affect your energy, choices become clearer.

- Morning yoga can boost digestion and metabolism so your body absorbs nutrients more effectively.
- A protein-rich breakfast supports sustained energy, and nutrient-dense meals with salmon, leafy greens, and vegetables provide stamina far longer than simple carbohydrates.
- You start to notice your cravings that might not be as healthy like an imbalance in your gut health or just a craving for being warm or connected.

- Noticing cravings, you recognize that you can restore energy and clarity through movement, fitness or yoga, or even listening to some good music.

Our choices and communication—both inner and outer—shape how we live and how we feel. Too much thinking can trap us in worry, and too much talking can pull us into drama. But when thought, expression, and action work together, we begin to grow in ways that feel grounding and meaningful. The ways we prepare food, move our bodies, rest, and recharge all become acts of care.

Then we begin to notice how The Healthy & Fun Choices Way is self-love, and it is woven through every one of these choices that creates us who we are to be today.

Here's a scenerio of how when we become more aware of what we can do, we let our fears drop just a little bit so we can just show up. I once had a friend who insisted he would never try yoga. I encouraged him to give it one chance. Afterward, he told me it changed his life. Breath, gentle movement, and mindful conversation can shift how we experience our bodies, our minds, and our daily lives. So many of us hold ourselves back before we begin, afraid of failure, judgment, or discomfort. Pain, fear, or old stories can stop us before we even start.

A friend of mine competes in Ironman triathlons, and after a hard fall that left her knees scraped and bleeding, she still got up and finished the race. Her perseverance reminds me that pain doesn't always mean stop—it can mean listen, soften, or adjust. The real work is discerning the difference between injury and the discomfort of growth.

Depression, on the other hand, can pull people inward until the bed feels like the only safe place. But even one small step—a short walk, a few stretches, or opening a window for fresh air—can shift the mind toward possibility. Joy often begins with movement, even the tiniest movement.

The Healthy & Fun Choices Way truly meets you where you are. People often say, "I can't do yoga because I can't touch the floor." But that limitation is the reason to begin. Using a chair, blocks, or the wall is not a sign of weakness—it's an act of awareness and self-respect. The same is true with physical pain. A sore foot left unmoved can stiffen and swell, while gentle, supported movement brings circulation and encourages healing.

There is a place for doctors, physical therapy, and counseling, and there is a place for self-care and self-love. True healing happens when we participate in our own care. When we listen to our bodies, honor their messages, and stay curious about what might help, we begin to live in partnership with our health instead of in fear.

Self-love guides us to take better care of ourselves—moving, breathing deeply, and giving our bodies rest. It helps us appreciate our bodies not for appearance, but for strength, flexibility, and function. Stretching, exercise, and mindful activity improve cardiovascular health, support muscles and bones, and reduce the risk of chronic illness. Movement releases endorphins—those "feel-good" hormones that lift mood, reduce stress, and support resilience.

Somewhere along the part of growth and falling in love with someone you may lose your own self-love and self-care. It is important that you don't because if you put the other person first, you aren't showing up the best for either of you. Self-love is a very important part of a relationship with another person.

A candle loses none of it's light by lighting another candle and that is the same with LOVE.

Love is the ability to connect with ourselves emotionally, physically, and spiritually. Love is getting to know ourselves. And when we understand self-love, we begin to nurture our emotions without judgment. This clarity helps us choose what supports us so we can show up more compassionately in every part of life.

Take a moment to reflect on what love means to you: What does Self-Love include?

What does it not include?

Researchers Eric Fields and Gina R. Kuperberg from Tufts University found that "positively biased self-views are a key component of healthy psychological functioning, influencing self-esteem, motivation, and determination." Self-compassion builds resilience—helping us recover from trauma, conflict, or failure more quickly.

As Oprah said, "You don't have to love yourself yet. But learning to like yourself will eventually lead to self-love." And that practice creates powerful biological changes; our brains respond to kindness, care, and safety.

The brain's chemistry—especially serotonin, endorphins, and dopamine—shapes our sense of well-being. When we treat ourselves with care, we stimulate the release of these powerful "feel-good" chemicals. Stress, overwork, and toxins can create oxidative stress, leading to inflammation, fatigue, and pain. But self-care reverses so much of this. Mindfulness, rest, nutritious food, and joyful movement all help calm inflammation and strengthen the immune system. When we nurture ourselves, we support emotional and physical health, reduce stress, and build resilience.

One of the clearest lessons I've learned from working with children, clients, and people of all ages is that abilities are always present—even when challenges make them harder to see. Dyslexia runs in my family, shaping creative approaches to learning and problem-solving. Friends who are blind remind us that vision is more than sight—it's awareness and connection. People who use wheelchairs show that movement comes in many forms. Stroke survivors reclaim independence step by step. And many with rare conditions like autism or cerebral palsy lead with joy, creativity, and expression in countless ways.

These experiences show that disabilities never define a person's worth. What matters is recognizing differences, offering support, and celebrating what we can do. Programs like Healthy & Fun Choices® are built on that foundation. Activities are created for participation, creativity, and joy—not perfection.

Going back to the first chapter when I was sharing about the relays I would lead in the workshops, you would see it in how creative participants were when asked to balance a banana while doing other actions. The focus is on the experience. In addition, adaptive tools and support amplify potential rather than spotlighting limits.

Life is full of possibilities when we focus on abilities first.
—Kirsten Klug

Take a moment to pause.

Part of recognizing a new way to redefine being healthy is being able to sit with this concept that maybe we really aren't broken when we have a disability, a disease or a dislike. Maybe we are just to learn in how we are.

Close your eyes, breathe slowly, and arrive in this moment. Think about where challenges have shown up—physical, emotional, or mental. Instead of labeling them as "disabilities," ask: What abilities are already here?

What strengths have these experiences revealed?

Write down one or two challenges, and next to each, list an ability or resource: a tool, a supportive person, a new perspective, a playful approach, or a strength discovered through experience. Consider how a small shift could make a big difference.

Let's try it here:

My "disability"	What "abilities" it has given me.
Aphasia	Learn how to get help to speak up
Dyslexia	Learned how AI can help me
Blindness	Realized my vision is more than sight
Stroke	Discovered new ways to move
TBI	I am more aware of my senses

Visualize yourself moving through the challenge with confidence and joy. Set one small intention for this week—something that helps you lean into ability, practice inclusion, or support accessibility for yourself or another. Remember, your abilities are unique and valuable.

When we focus on strengths, solutions, and creativity, we accomplish far more than we imagine. If you don't have any disabilities or set-backs, then maybe you can just imagine and put yourself in someone else shoes. Or maybe you can use this time to think about how you could offer help or listening for someone else. The most important part of wanting to help another person is first asking them how you can help. Try not to assume or think that your help is what they want or need.

Let's Play: Tree Pose (with Adaptations)
Stand tall with legs together, arms by your sides.

If you are seated or use a wheelchair, ensure the chair or wheels are stable. Bring your hands to your heart.

Feel your left foot grounding into the floor.

Lift your right knee and place your foot along your calf or thigh—avoiding the knee joint.

Let the knee gently open to the side.

Focus on a steady spot. Inhale, lifting your arms upward like branches reaching for sunlight. Lead with your heart center.

Use a wall or chair for support if needed. Exhale fully.

Lower your arms and leg.

Repeat on the other side.

    As you balance, notice how your body supports you. Whether you use a wall, chair, or your own focus, every adaptation reminds you that abilities come in many forms.

Balance isn't about perfection—it's about showing up, leaning into support, and celebrating the strength that is already within you.

Chapter 11

Rest and Restore

Sleep is one of the most powerful healing tools we have—and yet it's often the first thing we sacrifice. When you love yourself, you begin to understand that sleep is not lazy or optional; it's part of staying strong, creative, and emotionally balanced.

In my early design years, I was fueled by passion and deadlines. My programmer and I would trade projects at three or four in the morning—his start of day, my finish line. It was exciting, but I eventually learned that sleep deprivation made even fun work feel heavy. My creativity dulled, and conversations got foggy. It wasn't until I made sleep a priority that I noticed how much better I felt, thought, and designed.

Then came parenting. Babies, toddlers, school schedules—each phase demanded a new rhythm. It was a constant dance of adapting my sleep patterns to our family's needs. Every stage of life teaches something new about rest.

Why Rest Matters
Sleep gives the body a chance to repair, rebuild, and recharge. Muscles relax, tissues heal, memories settle in, and the nervous system resets. It's how the body catches up after everything you've asked of it during the day.

Healing after surgery or a brain injury depends on rest. During deep sleep, blood flow increases to muscles and tissues, bringing nutrients that help repair damage. I've met people who've recovered from comas or serious injuries and shared how their mind kept working quietly to heal while their body rested. Sleep is an active process of recovery, not an idle one.

Even athletes know this. After a marathon or race, the stretching and cool-down are essential, but it's that deep, long sleep afterward that truly restores the body. The same applies to anyone juggling stress or long workdays—sleep is where your strength regenerates.

The environment matters too. A good sleep setup invites healing. A quiet, dark, uncluttered space signals your brain to rest. Calming colors, cozy textures, and comfortable bedding make a difference. Whether you prefer a firm mattress or a soft one, what matters most is waking up without aches or stiffness. Some people like switching between different pillows for neck support, or even rotating bedding for a fresh feel.

Maybe you can relate: that sharing one big comforter doesn't always work. I'd have hot flashes and throw mine off while he piled his on. We switched to separate bedspreads—problem solved! It's funny how small adjustments make a big impact.

Hugs and cuddles help too. Physical connection—whether it's with a loved one or a pet—releases oxytocin, the "feel-good" hormone that calms the heart and reduces stress. But when you're recovering from surgery or managing a wound, even a sweet pet might be too much. Balance comfort with what your body truly needs.

Rest heals.
    It's how your body says
             "THANK YOU"
                    for showing up today. - Kirsten Klug

The Awkward Side of Sleep

Let's face it—sleep can get awkward. I've snored so loudly that girlfriends stopped inviting me on weekend trips!

Now, thanks to my sleep apnea machine and mouth retainers, I sleep better (and quieter), but I still get anxious about it when I go on trips or stay in a cabin. Luckily, the friends that truly matter invite me on the fun adventures like to Disneyland, the beach, the mountain ski trips, the cabin at Black Butte Ranch, and the rafting camping trips. Lucky for me my kids say it is a sound they enjoy hearing, as it means I am alive!

Camping adds another layer of adventure. Sleeping on a thin mat while the tent flaps in the wind or the dog snores at the door can make rest feel impossible—but also kind of funny. Hammock camping, though, changed everything. Hammocks lift your head and feet, relieve pressure points, and rock you to sleep.

One of my favorite spots for hammock camping was along the Rogue River. Two tall trees held my hammock perfectly. The night sky was clear, the river whispered nearby, and cool air settled around me. When the forecast hinted at rain, I added a tarp and net fly over the top and felt completely cocooned in comfort. Another time, on a road trip through Flagstaff, Arizona, we found a grove of aspens and set up hammocks beneath them. The air was crisp, the temperature perfect. A week later on that same road trip, we used an app called HipCamp and found a cattle farm with a grove of trees. Upon waking, baby cattle were roaming all around us!

One time on a rafting trip, my kids even turned three trees into a bunk-bed tower of hammocks—stacked right on top of each other! But I've also had experiences when the hammock or the tent was not the choice at all. Like the time we were camping on someones property in Colorado and as they left us at their special spot, she mentioned bears. That's when I chose the car and had troubles sleeping as my kids said they would be fine in their hammocks! Thankfully, they were just fine. No bears.

Being outside resets everything—our senses, our breathing, our natural sleep rhythm. Fresh air, natural sounds, and darkness without screens remind the body how to rest again.

Common Sleep Challenges
Sleep apnea causes breathing pauses that break up rest and sap energy. If I forget my CPAP even one night, I can tell the next morning—words come slower, and my thoughts feel hazy.

Snoring is common, but it can disrupt everyone's sleep. Restless Leg Syndrome makes it hard to keep still and fall asleep. PTSD can bring nightmares or make light and sound feel too intense. Nocturia—waking up to use the bathroom multiple times—can stem from several causes, including sleep apnea. If any of these sound familiar, check with a healthcare provider or sleep specialist. Getting to the root of the problem can make an enormous difference in how you feel each day.

When your body recognizes that it's safe and comfortable, sleep comes naturally.

Creating Your Sleep Sanctuary
A good night's rest begins before your head hits the pillow. Start with small bedtime habits that tell your brain, it's time to unwind and focus on the rest you need:
- Brush your teeth, wash your face, and look in the mirror with gratitude—you made it through another day.
- Turn down the lights and write down one or two things you're thankful for.
- Keep your room cool, around 65 degrees for most people.
- Use soft, cozy bedding or a weighted blanket that feels like a gentle hug.
- Close blinds or wear a sleep mask to block light.

- Try soft sounds: meditations, gentle music, or a brain-tapping audio that slows your breathing.
- Please keep your phone out of reach. Give yourself permission to disconnect.
- Your room should feel like a sanctuary, not a workspace.

Healthy sleep doesn't mean perfection—it means paying attention. Maybe your ideal bedtime routine is reading, a warm bath, or a short meditation. My mom likes Sudoku; my dad reads. My kids listen to music. My cat finds the perfect spots whether it is inside a box, on a window ledge or on a soft fluffy blanket right where I am to go to bed. Find what soothes you.

Most importantly remember that sleep restores creativity, balances emotions, and gives you energy to share your best self with the world. If your body or brain say I could use a fifteen minute nap... just take one! And, fall into the concept that every night is a fresh start—a time to reset and recharge.

Meditation Practices

Listening to meditations helps calm the nervous system, creating a gentle shift from stress into ease. Even a few minutes of guided breathing or visualization can refresh the mind, soften tension in the body, and make space for clearer thinking. Over time, meditations become a supportive practice—helping people feel more grounded, present, and able to respond to life rather than react to it.

You can listen to meditations that walk you through a series of imaginary concepts that can take you to locations that bring peace and stillness. Often the person leading the meditation will help you relax your body and soften your gaze. You can do meditations sitting up or laying down. Meditation is more than just relaxation, it is a healthy practice.

With meditation practice I can:
- Quiet the constant chatter of the mind. With time and repetition, thoughts settle, leading to greater clarity, focus, and inner stillness.
- Strengthen compassion and emotional balance. It helps you develop patience, empathy, and the ability to respond to life without being driven by fear, anger, or ego.
- Rewire the brain. Scientific studies show long-term mediators have changes in brain regions linked to attention, stress reduction, and emotional regulation.

Here's one of my favorite meditations that I wrote and share with you today for rest and peace.

Bird Nesting Meditation
Imagine you're a bird looking for the perfect place to build your nest. Choose what kind of bird you want to be—maybe a robin, an eagle, a hummingbird, or one that only exists in your imagination. Now, find the perfect spot: perhaps high in a tree, near a river, or tucked into soft moss.

Notice the smells and colors around you—the flowers, the air, the sounds of water or wind. Begin to gather what you need to build your nest: twigs, leaves, bits of fabric, maybe even a memory or story that feels meaningful. Weave everything together gently, piece by piece, until you created your safe and warm nest.

When your nest feels complete, imagine climbing in. Feel the support beneath you. Take a slow inhale and a long exhale. Let your shoulders soften down and back. Feel your heart settle. You are surrounded by love and understanding. You are at peace.

When you're ready, take one more deep breath and thank yourself for this moment of stillness. Rest is healing. It's how we recharge, restore, and reconnect with who we are.

Chapter 12

Food as Fuel

One rainy, blustery day after getting my kids off to the school bus, I realized I was cold and craving a hot mocha. I jumped in my car and drove down the street.

I saw our neighbor who goes running every single day regardless of the weather. Thinking about his choice and my choice, I kept driving but wondered which one of us would stay warm the longest. I ordered my drink and started sipping it as I drove back over the hill. The drink tasted great and when I got to the top of the hill I realized in about five minutes, my drink was gone! Then as I turned into my driveway, my neighbor was running by, so I rolled down my window and I said, "it is so impressive that you go running in this cold and wet weather!" He said with a big grin, "I am warm now and I can only get so wet."

His remark made me realize it is so true, we can only get so wet and fitness is a great way to care for our bodies. I share this with you in the food section because food is our fuel to keep our bodies moving and warm. Without our water and food intake, we would not last. At the same time, we often eat more calories than our body burns. It is important to keep that in mind.

Calories in and calories is a good way to track what you need. And you must think about the kind of calories going in. Packaged foods indicate calories on their packaging. For fruits, vegetables and meats, you can look online for a general idea of how much each of your fresh foods relate in calories.

How do you determine how much food you need to eat?

Do you eat three or five times a day because that is what you did growing up? Or are you mindful of when and what to eat based on what activities you have going on?

So many good questions can lead to so many good choices to be made around our food intake.

Food is a big part of our day and yet sometimes we barely make time for thinking about it. I learned a lot about food intake while healing from major surgeries. When I was resting in bed for months it was important to eat foods that kept my bowels moving and inflammation reduced, that way I was able to heal more. For instance, cancer patients or people with diabetes, thyroid or auto-immune diseases often benefit from meeting with a nutritionist or dietitian that can help with meal planning and how your meals interact with your medicines, as well as your therapies and movement to get you back to your new normal.

It might be convenient to go out to a coffee shop, but a flavored coffee at a popular coffee shop can now easily cost between $5-15 just for one 16 ounce drink that is gone in a few sips. I'll never forget when my daughter saw a TikTok and wanted to order this special drink. I almost passed out when I heard what was in it and how much it cost. Let me tell you it gave her that sugar high and the hormonal lows. Lesson learned. At home we can make quite a few cups of coffee for that same price and we know what is going in the drink. If you actually look at the amount of time that it takes to drive to the location to order the drink and the cost of gas to drive there, you will see that the cost is even more with your time and fuel.

Many people often say they eat healthy foods, yet eat out a lot. Eating out at restaurants can be a nice way to get together with others, at the same time you often do not know what is actually being put into the dishes. The healthiest meals are most often: fresh colorful foods cooked in your own kitchen. It's also important to think about how you eat and what priorities you put on your meals. Do you prepare your food and then take time to serve it at a table? Do you sit down together and have conversations over the meals? Do you just grab and go? Maybe even eat while you watch or interact with your phone or the screens?

I have found that it is important to be mindful about planning, preparing, serving and eating meals every day. When we can think ahead and purchase food that can use left-overs for the next meal or foods that complement each other, we can choose foods that nourish our soul and our body.

Making time to prepare and serve food together also provides a great opportunity to connect with family members and get caught up on activities or funny conversations over the enjoyment of a meal. I like to include my children in the planning and grocery shopping, too. It teaches them skills they will use for their lifetime. My 20 year old daughter loves to cook now that she is on her own. She also got such good ideas from working at a restaurant that made fresh foods.

Food serves as fuel for our body, brain, and soul, providing the necessary nutrients for optimal functioning. Understanding the role of nutrition and consuming nourishing foods is essential for overall health and well-being.

Here's how The Healthy & Fun Choices Way contributes to the concept of food as fuel:

Honoring Nutritional Needs: When you love yourself, you prioritize your well-being, including your nutritional needs. Self-love involves recognizing that your body deserves to be nourished with wholesome foods that provide essential nutrients. By honoring your nutritional needs, you can make choices that promote vitality and overall health.

Mindful Eating: Practicing self-love involves cultivating mindfulness in all aspects of life, including eating. Mindful eating is about being present and paying attention to the experience of eating. It involves listening to your body's hunger and fullness cues, savoring each bite, and being aware of the impact of food on your body and well-being. By practicing mindful eating, you can develop connection with choices that truly nourish you.

Individualized Nutrition: Each person has unique nutritional needs based on factors such as age, gender, activity level, and health conditions. When you love yourself, you recognize the importance of personalized nutrition and finding what works best for you. This involves understanding your body's responses to different foods, experimenting with various dietary approaches, and seeking professional guidance if needed. By tailoring your nutrition to suit your individual needs, you can optimize your body's functioning and support your overall well-being.

Balanced Approach: We emphasize balance and moderation in all aspects of life, including food choices. It means allowing yourself to enjoy a wide variety of foods while also being mindful of their nutritional value. Instead of restrictive or guilt-inducing behaviors around food, self-love promotes a positive and balanced approach, where nourishing foods are celebrated, and occasional indulgences are enjoyed without judgment. This balanced approach fosters a healthy relationship with food and promotes sustainable habits for long-term well-being.

Emotional and Soul Nourishment: When we encompasses nurturing not just the physical body but also the emotional and soulful aspects of ourselves, food can play a role in emotional well-being and provide comfort, pleasure, and connection.

Healthy & Fun Choices promotes these specific ideas around Food as Fuel: Look at your caloric intake and how much you burn with your work and exercise. If you notice that you are overeating or not making good choices for what your body needs, here are a couple ideas you can try:
- Reduce the size of your plate that you eat your meals on.
- Notice when you eat and make sure that you are getting protein and healthy foods in the morning.
- Reduce the amount of sugars you consume to zero and replace with healthy fats and oils, like Olive Oil, that your body might actually be craving for regeneration.
- Drink water first before consuming any other drinks like tea, coffee, milk, etc.
- Add micro-nutrients and vitamins to make sure you are getting the vitamins your body, brain, eyes, skin, cells

Pick Colorful Foods: Learn how the colors of food contribute to what your body needs. Explore the color charts and variety of food options that you have for each color of food. I say, look at your plate and ask yourself "what colors do I see? You can have friends or family do this too. If I see more white food, then choose a more colorful food choice to add for the next meal."

Get Creative in the Kitchen: Enjoy the process of making, serving and eating food. It always surprises me how it doesn't take much time to make a meal at home. You can even put a dish together and while it is cooking be making a salad, doing the dishes or enjoying a conversation with a family member. It is often when we are rushed or do not take the time to eat, when we make poor choices. Cooking at home and around others can improve choices and the quality of food you eat. Fast foods and snacks-on-the-go are usually low in protein and high in sugars.

Eat on a Smaller Plate: At some point in our fast food world, as burgers increased in sizes so did the companies that manufactured our plate sizes for eating food. When our family reduced the size of the plates that we eat on, our sizes of our bellies reduced as well. Also it is not necessary to pile your food high to look like you are eating the most. If you want to appear like you are that hungry, take a look at why. If it is a cultural norm, figure out if you are burning the same calories that you take in. If not, make some adjustments and see how you feel.

Have Fun with Your Food Choices: Try new foods each week—dragon fruit, kiwi, star fruit, raspberries, kale, spinach, the list goes on. What is a food that looks interesting to you or is in a recipe you have wanted to try?

Food is an important part of your monthly, weekly and daily plan. I like to choose my foods by the seasons and try to eat foods that are more common to the place that I live. Knowing where your food comes from and what ingredients are sourced from where is also helpful in ensuring that there are not extra hormones added to the foods. When we are able to eat local foods that are grown seasonally we also reduce the cost of fuel for shipping foods as well as encouraging the support of our local farmers.

One more important part to the food that you eat is knowing more about how it was grown. Sometimes we can't even tell if the fruits or vegetables were sprayed with chemicals or had altered growing cycles shortened to keep up with the demand. When this happens, our soil and food may be missing particular micro-nutrients, vitamins and minerals that our bodies need to keep our mind, eye, heart, nerve and cellular structures working well. After my near death experiences and coming back to life with brain injuries, I realized that I can empower positive change in how my body and brain heals by paying attention to what micro-nutrients I consume. I found MicroDaily EMF and highly recommend taking it in addition to the colorful foods you consume. Not only is it research-based, it was also developed for our Army to protect them from stress and electromagnetic fields like what we experience with our cell phones and computers.

Essential Water Consumption: They say that you should drink 8-10 glasses of water a day in addition to the coffee or other drinks you may have. I like to get in the habit of drinking water each time I am near a sink. Here's how I get my minimum of 8 glasses of water in a day: Right when I wake up in the morning, I have my 1st glass of water. Then, my 2nd glass is when I take my micro-nutrients and eat breakfast. My 3rd glass of water is around 10am, 4th glass at Noon, 5th glass around 2pm. My 6th container of water is taken during my yoga or work out at the gym. I have my 7th glass of water with dinner and then my 8th glass of water after dinner.

Mindful of Recycling, ReUsing and Reducing: In addition to consuming food, we also need to take into consideration how we are reducing, reusing, refusing, recycling, and re-purposing food and all the products food often comes in like films, containers, bags and boxes. Consider being part of a recycling program in your area. Remember you can often have a composting area for food and worms that vermicompost. Purchase just what you need to try to not waste too much. Recycling plastics, cans and cardboard is essential.

Use this space to brainstorm ideas on water intake, fresh foods, healthy eating, functional fitness ideas, activities, and whatever else you feel you want to journal...

Chapter 13

Eating By Color

Eating by Color is a concept that can help simplify what our body needs for people who can see colors. If you are blind or color blind, please ask for help and learn your tastes as colors.

The idea behind eating by color came to me when I was trying to lose weight after having my first child. I realized that colorful foods contained more nutrients and just by simply getting into a habit of looking down at my plate regarding what I was eating was a really easy way to be intentional. As my daughter began eating foods, too, I noticed that I talked to her about the different colors she was eating and soon she fell in love with vegetables. Still to this day colorful foods are her favorite! This easy way of eating is to encourage individuals to examine the colors of the foods on their plate. By doing so, you can assess the minerals, vitamins, proteins, and micro-nutrients and make adjustments in your next meal.

Rather than getting upset that you chose to many sugary or a coffee drink full of milk, you are able to just acknowledge it and simply adjust. There is less shame and guilt in eating and more joy in just living. And just as I began to notice the power of color on my own plate, I realized that cultures around the world have long celebrated this wisdom in their own beautiful ways.

A Celebration of Food, Culture & Connection
This concept of Eating by Color started around 2005, and it has been shared with many ever since. In 2009, I published the first Healthy & Fun Choices™ activity workbook to begin educating youth—because they are our future. Over time, I've realized the importance of this simple yet powerful idea, and I'm so glad that

you are learning it now, too. You can continue to share it with your family, friends, and everyone you come in contact with.

When we make meals a fun and engaging experience—maybe even turning it into a friendly challenge or creative game—we not only eat better, we remember more. Food becomes a story.

Native American tribes told stories around the foods they gathered and prepared so their children could pass down recipes and wisdom from generation to generation. Northern Europeans wove food into their holiday traditions, bringing families together in the kitchen to bake, share, and celebrate the changing seasons. The Mediterranean culture invites large families to gather around colorful plates filled with fresh vegetables, olive oils, grains, and herbs—each ingredient representing sunshine, soil, and sea.

In Asian cultures, color and balance guide every meal. The Japanese idea of go shiki—five colors: red, yellow, green, white, and black—creates harmony in both beauty and nutrition. In China, foods are chosen for their energy—warming, cooling, yin, or yang—reminding us that balance can be both seen and felt. Across Thailand and Vietnam, bright herbs and spices like basil, chili, turmeric, and lemongrass bring both vibrancy and vitality to every dish.

In India, food is a sacred act—a blend of devotion, color, and awareness. Golden turmeric, red chili, green coriander, and fragrant cardamom each tell a story of healing and connection. The Ayurvedic tradition teaches us that every color feeds not just the body but also the senses and the spirit.

To eat with awareness is to honor the life that grows from the earth and flows through us. -Kirsten Klug

When we look across all these traditions—from Native storytelling to European celebration, Asian balance, Mediterranean joy, and Indian mindfulness—we see the same truth:
Food connects us. Colors nourish us. Awareness transforms the way we eat.

Take a Mental Assessment
Each time you eat, take an assessment of all the colors you are eating. Take note if you see a lot of one or two colors and decide what color you could add into your next meal. Each day challenge yourself to eat as many colors of the rainbow as possible. By incorporating Eating by Color into our daily routine, we promote a healthy and balanced diet while fostering a sense of excitement and involvement among family members.

When you recognize that you avoid greens or meats or whatever it is, then take note and add that in as a supplement, mix or hide them in like in a smoothie, which allows you to taste it less.

Here are some examples of foods categorized by color, along with the nutrients, minerals, and vitamins typically found in each group. Turn a couple of pages to see more about why nutrients, minerals and vitamins are important to your wellbeing.

RED
Tomatoes: Rich in lycopene, vitamin C, and potassium.
Strawberries: Great for vitamin C, manganese, and antioxidants.
Raspberries: High in fiber, vitamin C, and antioxidants.
Grapes: Contain resveratrol, antioxidants, and vitamins C and K.
Rhubarb: Good source of vitamin K, calcium, and dietary fiber.
Cherries: Rich in antioxidants, vitamin C, and potassium.
Meats: Provide essential proteins, iron, and vitamin B12.

ORANGE

Oranges: High in vitamin C, folate, and fiber.
Kumquats: Rich in vitamin C, vitamin A, and fiber.
Small tomatoes: Contain vitamin C, vitamin A, and lycopene.
Apricots: Good source of vitamin A, vitamin C, and dietary fiber.
Sweet potatoes: Vitamin A, vitamin C, and potassium.

YELLOW

Bananas: Provide potassium, vitamin B6, and dietary fiber.
Pineapples: Rich in vitamin C, manganese, and bromelain.
Mustard: Contains dietary fiber, calcium, and iron.

GREEN

Spinach: High in iron, vitamin A, and vitamin K.
Kale: Packed with vitamin K, vitamin C, and antioxidants.
Celery: Contains vitamin K, vitamin C, and dietary fiber.
Cucumbers: vitamin K, vitamin C, and hydration.
Apples: Provide fiber, vitamin C, and antioxidants.
Artichokes: Rich in fiber, vitamin C, and foliate.

BLUE

Blueberries: High in antioxidants, vitamin C, and dietary fiber.
Plums: Rich in Vitamin C and dietary fiber.

PURPLE

Potatoes: Contain potassium, vitamin C, and dietary fiber.
Eggplant: Rich in dietary fiber, antioxidants, and foliate.

BROWN

Potatoes: Provide potassium, vitamin C, and dietary fiber.
Brown rice: Contains dietary fiber, magnesium, and selenium.
Beans: Rich in protein, dietary fiber, and minerals.

BLACK
Black beans: Protein, dietary fiber, and antioxidants.
Olives: Contain healthy fats, vitamin E, and antioxidants.

WHITE
Rice: Provides carbohydrates, B vitamins, and some minerals.
Pasta: Contains carbohydrates, dietary fiber, and B vitamins.

    Sauces may vary in color and nutrients depending on ingredients used. Remember, this is just a general overview, and the nutrient composition may vary depending on factors such as variety, ripeness, and cooking methods. It's always beneficial to choose a variety of colorful foods to ensure a diverse, nutrient-rich diet.
    Nutrients are the building blocks that keep our bodies running smoothly, like fuel for a well-tuned engine. They give us the energy to think, move, and create while supporting every tiny cell in the body. When we eat a variety of whole foods, we give our bodies the tools they need to repair, grow, and thrive. Think of nutrients as your body's personal toolkit—without them, it's hard to keep everything in working order.
    Vitamins are like your body's behind-the-scenes cheerleaders, quietly making sure all the important processes get done. They help turn food into energy, boost your immune system, and keep your skin, eyes, and nerves healthy. Vitamin C helps to fight off sickness and Vitamin D keeps your bones strong. Vitamins have a big impact on how vibrant and resilient we feel.
    Minerals are the strong framework that helps keep everything balanced in the body. They ensure your heart beats steadily, your muscles contract smoothly, and your brain sends the right signals. Calcium and magnesium, for example, help keep bones strong and prevent muscle cramps, while iron carries oxygen

through your blood. Without the right balance of minerals, your body's "wiring" can get a little frayed, leaving you feeling tired.

There are a series of foods that I call **Ingredients for Life**. They provide advantages for living a long life and can often help you gain a super power in the moment, here are some of them...

Pickled cucumbers and vegetables offer several advantages, including their ability to help with cramps and rehydrate a person who is dehydrated. When cucumbers and other vegetables are pickled, they undergo a fermentation process that enhances their nutritional value.

Here are some specific benefits of pickled or fermented foods:

Electrolyte balance: Pickled cucumbers and vegetables are often made with a brine solution that contains salt. Salt is rich in electrolytes, such as sodium and potassium, which are essential for maintaining proper fluid balance and preventing dehydration. Replenishing electrolytes can help alleviate muscle cramps that can occur due to electrolyte imbalances.

Hydration: Dehydration can result from various factors, including excessive sweating, illness, or insufficient fluid intake. Pickled vegetables, due to their high water content, can aid in rehydration. The water in pickled cucumbers and vegetables helps restore fluid levels in the body, contributing to overall hydration. Probiotics and digestion: Fermented pickles contain beneficial bacteria known as probiotics. These probiotics support a healthy gut microbiome and aid in digestion. They can improve the balance of gut bacteria, enhance nutrient absorption, and promote regular bowel movements.

Now, let's explore a simple recipe for refrigerator pickles using white vinegar, water, seasonings, and vegetables:

Ingredients for Refrigerator Seasoned Pickles:
- 2 cups white vinegar
- 2 cups water
- 2 tablespoons salt
- Seasonings of your choice (e.g., dill seeds, mustard seeds, garlic cloves, red pepper flakes)
- Fresh pickles and or vegetables of your choice

Instructions:
1. In a saucepan, combine the white vinegar, water, and salt. Bring the mixture to a boil, stirring until the salt dissolves.
2. Remove from heat and let it cool.
3. Prepare your vegetables by washing and slicing them into desired shapes. If using cucumbers, consider cutting them into spears or slices.
4. In a clean glass jar or container, place your chosen seasonings at the bottom. Add the sliced vegetables, packing them tightly but without crushing them.
5. Pour the cooled vinegar mixture over the vegetables, ensuring they are fully submerged.
6. Close the jar or container tightly and refrigerate. Allow the pickles to sit in the refrigerator for at least 24 hours to develop their flavors. The longer they sit, the more flavorful they become. Once pickled to your desired taste, you can start enjoying your refrigerator pickles. They can be stored for several weeks.

Feel free to adjust the seasonings and ingredients based on your preferences. Experiment with different vegetables and spice combinations to create unique and delicious pickles.

CLEAR: The Importance of Water... Drinking an adequate amount of water is crucial for maintaining good health. It is often recommended to consume 8-10 glasses, or about 64-80 ounces, of water per day. Here are some reasons why this daily water intake is important:

Hydration: Water is essential for proper hydration. Our bodies rely on water to carry out vital functions, such as regulating body temperature, lubricating joints, and aiding in digestion. When we don't consume enough water, dehydration can occur, leading to symptoms like fatigue, dizziness, and decreased cognition.

Nutrient absorption: Water plays a vital role in the absorption of nutrients from the food we eat. It helps break down nutrients and assists in their transportation to cells throughout the body. Without adequate water intake, nutrient absorption may be compromised, affecting overall health and well-being.

Waste elimination: Drinking enough water supports the proper elimination of waste products from the body. Water helps flush out toxins, aids in digestion, and promotes regular bowel movements. Insufficient water intake can contribute to constipation and hinder the body's natural detoxification processes.

Joint and muscle health: Adequate hydration is essential for maintaining healthy joints and muscles. Water acts as a lubricant for joints, facilitating smooth movement and reducing the risk of joint pain and stiffness. It also helps cushion and support muscles, promoting optimal performance during activities.

Skin health: Staying properly hydrated is beneficial for maintaining healthy and vibrant skin. Water helps moisturize the skin, improve its elasticity, and promote a youthful appearance. It can also help flush out toxins that may contribute to skin issues like acne and dryness.

Energy levels: Dehydration can cause fatigue and a lack of energy. By drinking enough water and getting your vitamins, nutrients, proteins and micro-nutrients throughout the day, you can help combat tiredness and improve your overall energy levels. Water supports proper blood circulation, delivering oxygen and nutrients to cells, which in turn boosts energy and promotes alertness.

Remember that individual water needs may vary based on factors like age, activity level, climate, and overall health. It's important to listen to your body's signals and drink water whenever you feel thirsty. Additionally, certain medical conditions or medications may require adjusting water intake, so it's advisable to consult with a healthcare professional.

By making it a habit of drinking enough water daily, you can support your overall health, maintain proper bodily functions, and enjoy the numerous benefits that hydration provides.

Infused Water Making Tips:
- Mix fruits, herbs, and spices to discover your favorite combinations.
- Start with warm water to help soak in the flavors/nutrients.
- Let ingredients steep for a couple of hours.
- Add ice cubes or refrigerate to enjoy cold.

Smoothie Making Tips:
- Use a blender or hand blender for smooth, creamy results.
- Let kids help by using a shaker or stirring manually—makes it fun and interactive.
- Try active twists: one workspace I promoted had a bike that blended smoothies as you pedaled! Fun and energizing.

Infused Water Ideas
- Lemon Mint: Sliced lemon + fresh mint leaves
- Cucumber Lime: Sliced cucumber + sliced lime
- Strawberry Basil: Sliced strawberries + fresh basil leaves
- Watermelon Mint: Cubed watermelon + fresh mint leaves
- Orange Blueberry: Sliced orange + fresh blueberries
- Pineapple Coconut: Chunks of pineapple + coconut water
- Raspberry Lime: Fresh raspberries + sliced lime
- Mango Ginger: Sliced mango + fresh ginger slices

Be mindful about how fruits contain natural sugars which can spike blood sugar or cause inflammation in some individuals. Feel free to customize these recipes by adding your favorite toppings like nuts, seeds, or a drizzle of honey. Enjoy these delicious, nutritious smoothies and protein shakes:

Smoothie & Protein Shake Ideas
- Berry Blast Smoothie: Mixed berries + banana + almond milk (+ honey/maple optional)
- Tropical Paradise Smoothie: Pineapple + mango + banana + coconut milk (+ spinach optional)
- Chocolate Peanut Butter Protein Shake: Chocolate protein powder + peanut butter + banana + almond milk
- Green Goddess Smoothie: Avocado + fresh spinach + banana + almond milk (+ honey/maple optional)
- Mocha Banana Protein Shake: Banana + cocoa powder + espresso + chocolate protein powder + almond milk
- Citrus Sunrise Smoothie: Orange + pineapple + mango + Greek yogurt
- Frog Smoothie: Avocado + banana + oat milk + honey
- Tropical Berry Shake: Strawberries + blueberries + pineapple + coconut milk

Start Your Day with Energy

Breakfast, often referred to as the most important meal of the day, holds a special significance. After an overnight fast, our body needs nourishment to kick-start the day. Eating a healthy breakfast provides us with essential nutrients, energy, and mental clarity. It sets the tone for the rest of the day by fueling our body and brain, aiding in concentration, and regulating our mood.

Skipping breakfast or prolonging the fasting period in the morning can have negative consequences. It may lead to low energy levels, decreased cognitive function, and a tendency to overeat later in the day. Breakfast helps stabilize blood sugar levels, preventing energy crashes and excessive snacking. It also supports a healthy metabolism and can contribute to weight management by reducing the likelihood of overindulging.

Moreover, breakfast provides an opportunity to incorporate nutrient-dense foods into our diet. Including sources of protein, whole grains, fruits, and vegetables in our morning meal supplies our body with vitamins, minerals, and fiber. These essential nutrients support our immune system, promote healthy digestion, and contribute to overall well-being.

While breakfast holds importance, it's essential to note that individual preferences and lifestyles can vary. Some people may prefer to practice intermittent fasting, which involves delaying the first meal of the day until later in the morning or early afternoon. This approach can have its own benefits, such as improved insulin sensitivity and fat burning. However, it's crucial to listen to your body and choose an eating pattern that fits your goals.

In summary, breakfast plays a vital role in providing the necessary nutrients and energy to start the day. It supports optimal cognitive e function, stabilizes blood sugar levels, and contributes to a balanced metabolism.

The questions can help you to start thinking about how to eat more intentional and be a mindful star:
- What color foods are you eating at each meal?
- Are you adjusting what you eat each day or do you tend to eat the same foods every day?
- Who do you eat with when you have a meal?
- Do you sit down with others or eat on your own?
- How long do you take to eat?
- Do you eat while on your phone or screen?

The Why Behind Mindfulness Eating

Plate size and mindful eating play a crucial role in our overall health and well-being. In 2009 when I started teaching Healthy & Fun Choices in schools, an organization called Reduce Screen Time helped me provide materials to school aged children and teachers so that we could start conversations around how much time youth and parents are on their screens. Our concern started a long time ago and now the cell phone goes almost everywhere with me and I have to be mindful to leave it when I eat, set it aside to charge in another spot when I sleep, and put it on a different counter when I eat a meal. Right now it is sitting next to me while I work here on my computer. Do you have places where you can put your cell phone to set it aside?

Avoiding distractions when we eat like computers, televisions, or gaming devices allows us to focus on our food, savor the flavors, and be in tune with our body's hunger and satiety cues. When we mindlessly eat, we may consume more calories than we need, leading to weight gain and potential health consequences. For instance if we are scrolling on our phones or watching Netflix and munching on popcorn or candy or whatever is available, we may eat more without even thinking about it. Some of this is okay, it's when it becomes and all the time or every day that it can be an issue.

Calorie counting can be a tool for individuals who want to stay in control of their calorie intake or reduce it for weight management purposes. By tracking the calories in the foods we eat, we can gain awareness of our energy consumption. However, it's important to approach calorie counting with caution. Obsessively focusing on numbers can lead to an unhealthy relationship with food and potentially develop or exacerbate disordered eating patterns. It's essential to prioritize nutrient-dense foods and overall balanced meals rather than solely fixating on calorie numbers. Exercise and physical activity can complement calorie control efforts by helping burn additional calories and supporting overall well-being.

Quantity of Food: When we eat on larger plates, we tend to serve ourselves larger portions, which can lead to overeating. By using smaller plates, we can visually trick our minds into perceiving a fuller plate and consume appropriate portions. Additionally, being mindful of our eating habits involves paying attention to our mealtime environment.

What are some thoughts that come up for you around the timing of when you eat, your plate size and mindfulness of eating?

My goal for you in this section of the book is to become more familiar with different ways of eating, so you are aware of the advantages and disadvantages. My way of eating is not necessarily a certain diet, but more of an intention to vary my colors, styles of cooking and spices.

Keto: The ketogenic diet is a low-carb, high-fat diet that aims to put the body into a state of ketosis, where it burns fat for fuel. Pros include potential weight loss, improved blood sugar control, and increased satiety. However, it can be restrictive, challenging to sustain, and may require careful monitoring of nutrient intake. Vegetarian: Vegetarianism involves excluding meat and seafood from the diet while allowing plant-based foods. Pros include potential health benefits, ethical considerations, and increased consumption of fruits, vegetables, and whole grains. However, it requires careful planning to ensure adequate intake of essential nutrients like protein, iron, and vitamin B12.

Paleo: The paleo diet focuses on eating foods believed to be consumed by our ancestors, such as lean meats, fruits, vegetables, nuts, and seeds, while avoiding processed foods, grains, and dairy. Pros include emphasizing whole, unprocessed foods and potential weight loss. However, it can be challenging to follow long-term, may limit nutrient diversity.

Mediterranean: The Mediterranean diet is inspired by the traditional eating patterns of countries bordering the Mediterranean Sea. It includes abundant plant-based foods, healthy fats, moderate fish and poultry, and limited red meat and processed foods. Pros include heart health benefits, emphasis on whole foods, and enjoyment of meals. However, portion control and mindful eating are important to prevent excessive calorie intake.

Pescatarian: Pescatarianism is a diet that includes plant-based foods along with seafood but excludes other animal meats. Pros include potential health benefits, increased omega-3 fatty acid intake from seafood, and environmental considerations. However, similar to vegetarianism, it requires attention to nutrient balance and potential supplementation of certain nutrients.

Whole30: Whole30 is a short-term elimination diet that focuses on whole, unprocessed foods for 30 days, excluding grains, dairy, legumes, added sugars, and processed foods. Pros include improved awareness of food choices, potential identification of food sensitivities, and resetting of eating habits. However, it is highly restrictive and may not be a long-term eating plan.

Vegan: A vegan diet excludes all animal products, including meat, dairy, eggs, and honey, focusing solely on plant-based foods. It is associated with potential benefits for health, animal welfare, and environmental sustainability, but careful attention is required to ensure adequate intake of certain nutrients like vitamin B12 and iron.

Flexitarian: The flexitarian diet is primarily plant-based but allows for occasional consumption of meat and other animal products. It offers the flexibility of a predominantly vegetarian diet while still incorporating some animal-based foods if desired.

DASH (Dietary Approaches to Stop Hypertension): The DASH diet is specifically designed to lower blood pressure and promote heart health. It emphasizes fruits, vegetables, whole grains, lean proteins, and low-fat dairy while limiting fats and sugars/sodium.

Inflammation-reducing diet: An inflammation-reducing diet focuses on consuming foods that help reduce inflammation in the body, which is associated with chronic conditions like heart disease, arthritis, and certain cancers. This diet emphasizes whole foods, such as fruits, vegetables, whole grains, healthy fats (like olive oil and avocados), and lean proteins, while minimizing processed foods, refined sugars, and trans fats. Including anti-inflammatory foods like fatty fish (rich in omega-3s), turmeric, ginger, and leafy greens can help and also have higher prices.

Fasting: Fasting involves voluntarily abstaining from food or caloric beverages for a specific period. Different fasting methods exist, such as intermittent fasting or time-restricted eating. Pros include potential weight loss, improved insulin sensitivity, and convenience for some individuals. However, it may not be suitable for everyone, and proper hydration and nutrient intake during eating windows are important.

While it is essential to address individual food sensitivities and make choices that support overall well-being, it is advisable to consult with a healthcare professional or registered dietitian to ensure nutritional adequacy and balance in the diet. The reason I wanted to share here is to start conversations around these because I believe that at the root of many diseases could just be allergies to the products or traces of plastics that we consume.

Regarding **nutritionists and dietitians**, both are trained professionals who specialize in food and nutrition. Nutritionists typically have a broad knowledge of nutrition and can provide general guidance. On the other hand, dietitians are registered and licensed professionals who have undergone specific education and training, including clinical nutrition therapy. They can provide more specialized advice, especially when dealing with medical conditions like cancer and the potential interactions between diet and medications. It is crucial for doctors and dietitians to collaborate in order to ensure a comprehensive approach.

Gluten-free: A gluten-free diet eliminates gluten, a protein found in wheat, barley, and rye. It is crucial for individuals with celiac disease or gluten intolerance to avoid gluten-containing foods to prevent digestive issues, skin problems, and other symptoms. To avoid gluten, one can choose gluten-free alternatives like rice, quinoa, corn, and gluten-free bread, pasta, and cereals.

Dairy-free: A dairy-free diet excludes all forms of dairy products, including milk, cheese, yogurt, and butter. This is important for individuals with lactose intolerance or dairy allergies. To replace dairy, one can opt for plant-based milk alternatives like almond, soy, oat, or coconut milk, and explore dairy-free alternatives like vegan cheeses and yogurts.

Soy-free: A soy-free diet avoids foods containing soybeans or soy products. To avoid soy, it's important to read ingredient labels carefully and look for alternatives like tofu, tempeh, soy milk, and soy sauce. Opt for alternative protein sources such as beans, lentils, quinoa, or meat/fish/poultry if suitable.

Phytoestrogen Sensitivity: Soy products (tofu, soy milk, edamame), flaxseed, sesame seeds, and certain legumes. For those who notice hormonal symptoms such as bloating, breast tenderness, mood changes, or irregular cycles, reducing these foods can help bring the body back into balance.

Sulpha-free: Sulfas are found in foods to preserve them. Wine is full of sulphas and can cause red cheeks to people who are sensitive to sulphites. Cosmetic and soap products, as well as many detergents also often have sulfites and sulphas integrated in and can cause skin rashes and blisters.

Nightshade Sensitivity: Some people are sensitive to nightshade vegetables, which naturally contain alkaloids that can irritate the gut or increase inflammation. Common nightshades include tomatoes, potatoes (not sweet potatoes), peppers, eggplant, and paprika. If someone notices joint pain, digestive discomfort, or skin irritation after eating these foods.

There are some diseases that have food sensitities to be aware of, here is a simplified list of them...

Pre-diabetes: Pre-diabetes is a condition in which blood sugar levels are higher than normal but not yet high enough to be diagnosed as diabetes. It is a warning sign that indicates increased risk for developing type 2 diabetes. To prevent the progression to diabetes, lifestyle changes such as adopting a healthy diet, engaging in regular physical activity, maintaining a healthy weight, and managing stress are crucial. Regular monitoring of blood sugar levels and routine healthcare check-ups are important.

Gestational diabetes: Gestational diabetes occurs during pregnancy when the body cannot produce enough insulin to meet the increased demands. It affects the way the body uses sugar and can potentially lead to complications for both the mother and the baby. Pregnant women are typically screened for gestational diabetes, and if diagnosed, they may need to monitor blood sugar levels, follow a specific meal plan, engage in regular physical activity, and, in some cases, take insulin. Close monitoring and regular prenatal care are essential for managing gestational diabetes and minimizing risks.

Diabetes type 1: Type 1 diabetes is an autoimmune condition where the immune system mistakenly attacks and destroys the insulin-producing cells in the pancreas. As a result, the body cannot produce insulin, requiring lifelong insulin therapy. Management of type 1 diabetes involves regular monitoring of blood sugar levels, insulin administration (through injections or an insulin pump), following a healthy meal plan, engaging in physical activity, and ongoing medical care.

Diabetes type 2: Type 2 diabetes is a chronic condition characterized by insulin resistance and high blood sugar levels. It is often associated with lifestyle factors such as obesity, sedentary behavior, and poor dietary choices. Prevention and management of type 2 diabetes involve adopting a healthy lifestyle, including a balanced diet rich in fruits, vegetables, whole grains, lean proteins, and healthy fats. Regular physical activity, weight management, blood sugar monitoring, and medication (if prescribed) are important components of managing type 2 diabetes.

It's important to note that each individual's diabetes management may vary, and personalized guidance from healthcare professionals, such as doctors and registered dietitians, is crucial. They can provide individualized recommendations on diet, exercise, medication, and self-care practices to effectively prevent or manage diabetes. Regular monitoring, education, and support are key for living a healthy and fulfilling life with diabetes.

Conversations around food choices are the key ingredient to sustainability and healthy living. Taking notes or making a food journal is one of the best ways to figure out your allergies and sensitivities. *Remember if you start a new medicine or have a limited immune system at different times of the year, your food sensitives may change.*

When it comes to how we support our body with liquids, here's an overview of some popular choices and their potential impact on your health.

Water: In general, water is the healthiest and most hydrating beverage choice. It's important to stay hydrated throughout the day by drinking an adequate amount of water. It's receommended that we drink 8-10 glasses of water today. If you ever are feeling exhausted or experiencing cramping, try to drink a little more water and see if that helps. Bring a water bottle with you to your activities. Set a glass next to your sink.

Tea: Tea, especially herbal and green teas, can be a healthy choice as they are rich in antioxidants and have potential health benefits. They can contribute to hydration and may offer calming or energizing effects, depending on the type of tea.

Coffee and Coffee Shops: Coffee can provide an energy boost and improve focus due to its caffeine content. It also contains antioxidants. However, it's important to moderate consumption, as excessive caffeine intake can lead to jitters, disrupted sleep, or increased heart rate. *Be mindful of added sugars, syrups, or high-calorie creamers in coffee shop drinks, as they can contribute to excess sugar and calorie intake.*

Sodas/Pop: Sugary sodas or soft drinks are typically high in added sugars and offer little to no nutritional value. Regular consumption of these beverages can contribute to weight gain, tooth decay, and increased risk of chronic diseases such as type 2 diabetes and heart disease.

Refreshers: Refreshers typically refer to flavored, often carbonated, non-alcoholic beverages. Their nutritional value varies depending on the ingredients. Some refreshers may contain added sugars or artificial sweeteners, so it's essential to read labels and choose options with minimal added sugars or opt for homemade alternatives with natural ingredients.

Alcohol: There is a lot of research lately connecting alcohol to cancers and often behaviors that do not support a healthy and fun lifestyle. You get to decide what you choose to drink. Alcoholic beverages have been around for a long time and alcoholism is more easily passed from one generation to the next, so please drink wisely.

Beer: Beer, when consumed in moderation, can be part of a balanced lifestyle. It contains alcohol and calories, so moderation is key. Excessive alcohol consumption can lead to various health issues, including liver problems, weight gain, and increased risk of accidents or alcohol-related diseases.

Wine: Moderate wine consumption has been associated with potential health benefits, particularly red wine due to its antioxidant content. It may offer cardiovascular benefits and contribute to relaxation. However, excessive alcohol intake can negate any potential benefits, so moderation is crucial.

Hard Liquor: Hard liquor, such as vodka, whiskey, or rum, contains higher alcohol content compared to beer or wine. Excessive consumption can have serious health consequences, including liver damage, addiction, and increased risk of accidents. It's important to drink responsibly and be aware of alcohol tolerance.

Energy drinks: These typically contain high amounts of caffeine, added sugars and other stimulants or herbal extracts. While these ingredients may provide a temporary energy boost, their long-term effects and safety are still being studied.

If you need an energy boost, try opting for natural options like black or green tea, which provide moderate amounts of caffeine along with antioxidants.

Staying hydrated with water, eating a balanced diet, getting enough sleep, and engaging in regular physical activity can help maintain energy levels throughout the day without relying on energy drinks.

If you have concerns about your caffeine intake or are looking for personalized guidance on choosing suitable beverages for your needs, it's advisable to consult with a healthcare professional or registered dietitian. They can provide you with individualized recommendations based on your health status and goals.

When it comes to recognizing potential issues with diets and eating disorders, it's important to be mindful:
- Drastic changes in weight: Significant weight loss or weight gain can be indicative of an underlying issue with the person's relationship with food.
- Obsession with body image: An excessive preoccupation

with body shape, size, or appearance, along with distorted body perception, can be warning signs of disorder.
- Restrictive eating patterns: Unusual dietary restrictions, such as eliminating entire food groups or extreme calorie counting, may suggest disordered eating behaviors.
- Skipping meals or avoiding social eating: Frequent avoidance of meals, making excuses to avoid eating with others, or isolating oneself during mealtime.
- Intense fear of gaining weight: If expresses a disproportionate fear of gaining weight or displays excessive guilt or shame after eating, it could indicate an unhealthy relationship with food.
- Excessive exercise: Compulsive or excessive exercise routines, especially when driven by a desire to "burn off" consumed calories, can be a sign of disordered eating.
- Changes in mood or behavior: Noticeable shifts in mood, increased irritability, social withdrawal, or heightened sensitivity to comments about food or appearance may suggest the presence of an eating disorder.
- Preoccupation with food, cooking, or recipes: An intense focus on food-related activities, such as cooking for others but not eating oneself, collecting recipes, or reading cook books obsessively, can be indicative of an eating disorder.

Remember, these signs may vary, and the presence of one or more doesn't necessarily confirm the presence of an eating disorder. If you observe these signs and they significantly impact physical and emotional well-being, it is crucial to seek professional help.

Encouraging open and non-judgmental communication, involving all ages in grocery shopping and food preparation can help everyone be more comfortable with food and drink choices.

Ingredients for Life

Our holidays were a symphony of smells and flavors. The warm, sweet aroma of Swedish rye bread rising in the oven would fill the entire house. Making it was a labor of love: punch it down, let it rise, punch it down again, until it reached the perfect texture. The subtle licorice note of anise would dance through the kitchen, and when the bread finally emerged, golden and fragrant, it carried with it the memory of grandparents, the legacy of generations, and the joy of family gathered around the table. Hard tack, those oddly shaped crackers with tiny bumps that somehow tasted heavenly when spread with butter, and melted Havarti cheese—small delights became treasures. Each recipe was more than a meal; it was a conversation across time, a way to touch the lives of ancestors, and a bridge for telling stories about who we are and where we come from.

Food carries culture with it. I've been lucky to experience the richness of other traditions as well. Holidays and family gatherings in Hispanic households are a burst of color and spice, where every dish tells a story and invites everyone to participate. The bayous of the South bring seafood to the center of life, fresh and flavorful, with flavors shaped by the land and water. Coastal families rely on the bounty of the ocean, and the Mediterranean has taught the world the joy of olive oil, fresh produce, and meals that honor both health and pleasure. Across the globe, we see the same pattern: food is more than nutrients—it's identity, history, and love.

As these cultural and family traditions taught me, food is also healing. Nutritionists and dietitians are allies in this journey, guiding us to make choices that support health during challenges. Allergies, illnesses, surgeries, and even everyday stress can all benefit from mindful food decisions. Learning how to combine flavors, ingredients, and nutrients is empowering. When we understand food as both medicine and pleasure, we reclaim agency over our own bodies and well-being.

Sometimes, the recognition we get around food is playful, social, and memorable. At potlucks and gatherings, people often become "famous" for a particular dish. My ex became legendary for his deep-fried donuts, golden perfection with a secret crunch that everyone anticipated. I became known for my colorful salads, where every bite carried texture, flavor, and a little joy. My friend, Polish and meticulous, earned her reputation through her finely chopped Polish potato salad—hours of preparation that revealed her care and commitment. These moments are more than ego or praise; they are reflections of identity and choice. What are you known for at gatherings? Does it reflect what you want to be known for, and does it honor the way you want to nourish yourself?

This is the beauty of Ingredients for Life: each meal, each tradition, each dish is an opportunity to tell a story and express your values. By thinking about the colors, textures, and nutrients in your food, you provide your body with the vitamins, minerals, proteins, carbohydrates, and micro-nutrients it needs to thrive. Watching how students, teachers, and families respond to these concepts over the years has been illuminating. When I shared the ideas through workshops, I could see the excitement in real time—the questions, the experiments in the kitchen, the joy of discovery. Over time, I witnessed how these ideas took root, how children used them to create meals for themselves, how they began to think about the colors on their plate, the balance of nutrients, and the stories behind what they were eating.

Food is not just fuel. It is connection, heritage, healing, and expression. It is a chance to celebrate who we are, what we love, and how we care for ourselves and others. As you explore your own culinary journey, take time to reflect, write down your favorite dishes, and consider recipes that carry personal meaning. Let your meals be playful, experimental, and nourishing. Let them teach you, surprise you, and bring you closer to the people around your table.

Because in the end, the ingredients we choose, the stories we tell through food, and the rituals we create are all part of the legacy we leave behind—for ourselves, our families, and those who will follow.

Use this space to write out what kind of legacy you would like to create:

Chapter 14

Being Proactive Over Reactive

Living with intention is about seeing your life as a whole while also embracing each small moment for what it is. Think of it like going on a hike—maybe the destination is the waterfall at the end of the trail, but part of the joy is noticing the birdsong, the crunch of leaves, the sunlight filtering through the trees. It's not just about the goal—it's about being present along the way.

When we take thoughtful actions that reflect what matters to us, rather than simply reacting to what is thrown at us, we have that ability to be proactive.

If we focus only on the outcome—on the reward or result—we can become discouraged or frustrated when things don't go as planned. But when we stay connected to the moment and the purpose behind what we're doing, we move with more grace, and fewer expectations.

Time, Distractions & Re-Aligning

For many of us, time management is both a skill and a challenge. You might get a lot done and still struggle with being on time. Maybe you plan well, but lose track of small things like how long it takes to find parking, or how long it takes to actually get out the door.

What helps is a simple mindset shift. Instead of aiming to arrive at 3:00 p.m., imagine being ready by 2:50. That gives you breathing room—to pause, take in your surroundings, maybe even stop to smell the flowers—and still ready for what's next. How are you doing with time these days?

Are your tools like cell phone or paper calendar working?

Do you ever feel rushed or relaxed?

Distractions are real, especially with phones, alerts, and endless screens.

It's easy to double-book or miss something. One helpful habit is to choose one calendar to be your main one—whether it's digital or paper—and make that your scheduling home base. Always check there first when making plans. And if you accidentally overlap events (because we all do sometimes), prioritize what aligns with your values, then kindly communicate and reschedule.

Tools to Help You Stay Centered and Aligned

Instead of diving into a long checklist, consider these ideas as gentle reminders to support your everyday rhythm. You don't have to do them all—pick one or two that feel helpful right now.

Planning Projects
- Break things into smaller steps—it helps you feel momentum.
- Set clear intentions for each step.
- Track your progress gently (a journal or timeline works).
- Give yourself time and space—not everything is urgent.
- Be flexible. Plans are guides, not rules.

Managing Time
- Focus on what's most important, not just what's loudest.
- Use tools that fit your style—whether that's a planner, an app, or sticky notes.
- Set aside focused time for key tasks.
- Ask for help or delegate when you can.
- Build in breaks. Your brain and body will thank you.

Communicating with Clarity
- Listen fully before responding.
- Keep your messages simple and thoughtful.
- Before sending, reread and imagine how it might sound to the other person.
- Don't rush replies—respond with care when you're ready.
- Be kind. Tone matters more than we realize.

Listening with Your Heart
- Show you're listening with your eyes, nods, and presence.
- Let people finish their thoughts before jumping in.
- Ask questions and reflect what you hear.
- Jot down notes if it helps you stay focused.
- Listening is a skill. And it deepens trust.

Avoiding Miscommunication
- Double-check times, names, and key info.
- Ask for feedback—not for validation, but to grow.
- Give yourself time to practice.
- Keep learning—words matter, and you deserve to express yourself well.

You don't have to be perfect. You just have to show up and that always allows to an ability to open up. - *Kirsten Klug*

All of these habits help make daily life flow with a little more ease and connection. They're not just "productivity tips"—they're ways to feel more grounded, more present, and more you.

In many homes, meaningful routines—like sharing meals, unplugging for a bit, or taking a walk—create chances to connect. Even doing dishes together or folding laundry can become quiet times for conversation or reflection.

Sometimes life calls us to make big decisions—like moving to a new city or shifting what "family" means. These moments are easier to face when we've practiced setting boundaries, taking care of ourselves, and trusting our ability to adapt.

Going through a divorce can be hard because it is new and different than what you have done before. Having conversations and even having moments that don't work or are frustrating are how we get to figuring out what does work. I am so proud of my family in how we have adjusted. At times I have been sad, mad and upset and yet I know in the long term it is what was needed for everyone in the situation. We chose to have the kids live with me so that they had consistency and were closer to the schools and farm where they attended.

The goal isn't to control everything. The goal is to live with awareness and choice. When you take action based on your intentions—rather than on urgency or pressure—you'll begin to feel a shift. Some of the ways you will feel this include:
- Life feels more aligned.
- Your energy flows more freely.
- You experience a little more joy in the process.

You've got this! What is one small way you can adjust so you can be more proactive than reactive?

Chapter 15

Leading with Intention

In this chapter, we are exploring the powerful connection between mindset, brain science, kindness, and learning to move forward with trust and intentional practice. These ideas can help you shape thoughts, take healthier actions, and respond to life with greater clarity and confidence knowing that life is a journey.

Let's start with mindset—the way you view yourself and the world around you. Research shows that your beliefs can directly influence how you think, feel, and act. Adopting a growth mindset, where you believe you can learn, adapt, and improve, opens the door to resilience. Challenges become opportunities, and setbacks feel less like failures and more like stepping stones.

Then, there's your brain—an incredible organ that's always changing. Thanks to something called neuroplasticity, your brain can actually rewire itself based on your experiences and the thoughts you focus on. This means that every time you practice gratitude, kindness, mindfulness, or even try something new, you're literally strengthening those areas in your brain.

One of the simplest ways to support your mindset and your brain is through kindness. Science shows that acts of kindness release oxytocin, the "feel-good" hormone that supports connection and emotional well-being. Whether it's a smile, a kind word, or helping someone out, these small moments can have lasting impacts—on others and on you.

But even with all of this knowledge, there are still hard moments—times when trust is tested. This is where forging forward in trust comes in. Trusting yourself, others, and the process doesn't mean having all the answers. It means being willing to take a step even when the outcome is uncertain. And it's that willingness that leads to growth.

Some people naturally seem confident in their decisions. Others struggle. The difference often comes down to how much we trust our choices. Trusting yourself doesn't mean everything will go perfectly—it just means you believe in your ability to learn, adjust, and keep going.

Think of it like this: trusting your choices means anchoring yourself in your values, your intuition, and your knowledge. When you trust yourself, you're more likely to stay focused through setbacks, more open to learning, and more confident in your ability to navigate change.

And just like mindset, trust is something you build. It comes with reflection, compassion, and learning from experience. It's something you practice—just like healthy habits, good communication, or making time for rest and play.

From Vision to Action
One helpful way to build trust and move forward is by starting with the end in mind. Picture the kind of person you want to become, the goals you want to reach, or the change you want to make. That vision can guide your steps and help you stay on track.

Many times I worked with coaches or mentors and they would have me write down my goal at the bottom of the page and then the steps to get there. I wanted to figure out what would happen if I changed the order, instead of going down what if I put the goal at the top of the page and worked up?

So I tried it and created this **GOAL** worksheet that you can try out and see if it helps you too. This is good for setting goals whether they are for a specific task or long-term.

The Top box is to write your **Goal**
Next in the box below write **Obstacles**
In the box below write the   **Actions** you can take
Then at the bottom indicate   **Life now** as you know it.

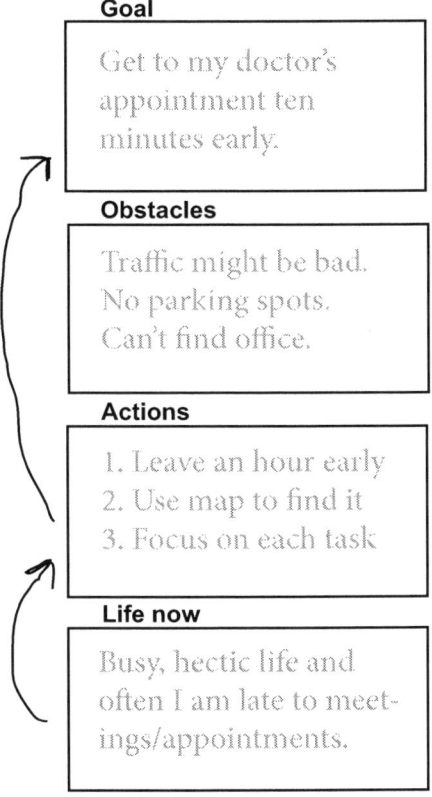

Above is an example because with Aphasia and brain injury it is hard to figure out timing when working towards a time stamp. This is how I make sure I get places on time now.

Start at the bottom LIFE NOW, then go up to your GOAL and OBSTACLES, and then write ACTIONS.

You may have to try this out a couple of times before it becomes easy for you to do. You can use it on any goal not just time management in the case that I gave here. This reflection can help you reconnect with your purpose and see your progress.

You can also use my framework that I created called **ACTION** it offers a more specific guide to getting things done now:

The **ACTION** approach is a practical framework for moving forward with goals efficiently:
- **Act:** Understand why the task or goal is important.
- **Calculate:** Estimate how long it will take and track progress.
- **Time** Schedule or Chunk: Break the task into smaller bits.
- **Intuition:** Trust your instincts when prioritizing.
- **Obstacles:** Identify potential barriers and plan.
- **Now:** Determine if right to act or schedule start time.

But here's the key: don't wait for everything to be perfect before you start. Small steps forward—even imperfect ones—build momentum. Practice **ACTION** right here...

Action: What's a goal you want to accomplish?

Calculate: When do you want it done? How much time today?

Time Schedule: What time will start it today?

Intuition: What does your intuition say right now?

Obstacles: What could get in your way?

Now: Can you start it now or when?

1. Let's go through a couple of examples so you can see how I use this. **ACTION** for getting my laundry done this Sunday while I am finishing the book:

Action: I want to get four loads of laundry done today.
Calculate: I need to separate them into piles and start them.
Time: It will take about an hour a load.
Intuition: I need to take breaks so this will be good.
Obstacles: I might forget since I can't see the laundry room.
Now: Set a timer on the hour. Go!

2. Take **ACTION** on Getting to the Gym Every Day:

Action: I want to just show up at the gym every day.
Calculate: It takes 20 minutes to get there and one hour there.
Time: I need to schedule a specific time for each day.
Intuition: My days are ever changing, that is why it gets missed.
Obstacles: Lame excuses get in my way.
Now: Schedule a morning and an evening time and pick one.

3. One more, how about **ACTION** Studying for a Test:

Action: I need to study for my upcoming test.
Calculate: Two hours to review chapters; one hour to study.
Time: Three hours total, but I could break it up.
Intuition: Smaller chunks will be less overwhelming.
Obstacles: So many fun things to do.
Now: Schedule time and fit fun activities between.

Aim for progress, it is the steps in a direction and as you take those steps you may adjust your goal or what is holding you back.

Recently I was listening to a podcast and the person being interviewed shared that it is often something we are holding onto from our past that could be holding us back. Maybe you still miss an old friend or something within an experience that as you have grown up you do less of that one thing.

With *The Healthy and Fun Choices Way* in mind you have options, you can sit with the sad or grieving parts witnessing them and knowing that you are listening. You could go out in nature for a refreshing walk. You could just take a break and play with your dog or kids and come back at a certain date or time you pick. Or when I teach yoga, this is where I encourage you to come back to your breath, notice your inhale and your exhale,

Then, think about what you could do to make it easier. What could you let go of?

How can you lead more with your heart?

Inhale and exhale. Come back to your breath and just be present. In slowing down to what is, we are often able to let go more and find our way.

Being present is a gift in itself. -Kirsten Klug

Building a Positive Life from the Inside Out
Part of this process includes creating space to live well.
How do you want to live?

What do you like to surround yourself with that will make you feel at peace and allow you to smile. I like to think about all of the senses when I create a positive, uplifting space. I choose colors, paintings, scents, textures, furniture design, spacial openness and so on. I know that we can't always get exactly what we want, we may get free items just to get by at certain points in our life. Even when it isn't perfect or just what you would like, I bet you can find something little that would support you and make you smile. I have a ceramic flower that I created when I was in college in art school. Even when everything isn't right, I am able to connect with that flower.

In addition to how you design the space that you live in, you also want to try to choose to surround yourself with supportive people, setting healthy boundaries, and saying no to situations that don't align with your values. It means loving yourself enough to protect your time and energy.

Learning to Set Healthy Boundaries
For many years, our life looked solid from the outside. We built a beautiful home, raised children, grew a business, played in sports leagues, spent time with friends, and even managed vacations. On paper, it seemed like we had created the kind of life most people hope for. But beneath the surface, there was a constant pressure—an undercurrent of feeling like what I did was never quite right or never quite enough. No matter how well things seemed to be going, there was always something to fix, improve, or worry about, especially around money.

Over time, that strain built the way heat builds beneath a pot. At first it simmers quietly. Then it becomes a rolling boil. And eventually, it creates enough steam to power a locomotive. That's what happened inside me: the pressure reached its tipping point, and I realized something fundamental needed to change.

When I created a home of my own with my children, the contrast was immediate. The house felt lighter, calmer—like it exhaled right along with us. I noticed how grounded I felt choosing paint colors, hanging artwork, and setting up our spaces without second-guessing myself. Even simple things, like leaving dishes in the sink after a long day, suddenly felt human instead of "not good enough." That was the moment I understood just how much emotional weight I had been carrying.

Setting healthy boundaries became essential. One of the first was adjusting our routines so that pick-ups and drop-offs happened at the curb rather than at the door. That small shift protected the peaceful environment I was building and helped me feel confident in my own home again. Little choices added up—trusting my style, creating systems that worked for us, and allowing myself to prioritize what felt genuine and sustainable.

Even my sleep changed. For years, I slept lightly, shifting and adjusting around someone else's needs. Once I created more space—physically and emotionally—I finally slept through the night. Waking up rested felt like reclaiming a part of myself I didn't even realize I had lost.

These changes weren't dramatic on the surface, but together they formed a turning point. By noticing the pressure, listening to my own needs, and setting boundaries that honored them, I created room for more clarity, ease, and joy—one intentional choice at a time. Asking permission before giving feedback is one simple way to practice this. For example, instead of blurting out, "That picture is crooked," you might ask, "Would you like some feedback?" If the answer is yes, share. If it's no, hold your thought.

I even teach kids this idea in classrooms. We imagine our heads like jars filled with all our wonderful ideas. The lid stays on until it's the right time—like when we raise our hand or ask permission. Then, when it's time to share, we "open the jar" and let our idea fly out. It helps remind us that we don't have to say everything we're thinking the moment it pops into our minds.

The truth is, some relationships or habits can be draining, negative, or even toxic. Recognizing that—and letting go when needed—is part of creating a healthier, more joyful life. Choosing positive habits like daily movement, screen-free time, nourishing meals, and emotional self-care makes all the difference. Healthy boundaries create room for trust, respect, and better communication. And when those things grow, so does connection.

This is something I've lived through. My accident became a turning point. I realized I had the power to choose healing. I changed my mindset, prioritized anti-inflammatory foods, drank more water, and worked with many therapists who helped me find strength and I focused on what I could do on my own to help in so many areas like occupational, physical, vision, psychological, neurofeedback, speech and brain therapy—to heal my voice, my thoughts, and my relationships. I realized that in some cases when you go through really tough situations you don't recover fully, rather you grow and change into a new you.

The biggest takeaway? Being proactive means you take responsibility for you—your joy and your path forward.

Expanding so you can Trust Again
By learning to trust yourself, nurture your mindset, and take meaningful action, you're not only creating a better life for

yourself—you're also becoming the kind of person who inspires and supports others. That's what The Healthy & Fun Choices Way is all about.

One way you can use the proactive mindset over being reactive, is when something goes differently than you imagined. Here are examples you can think about and practice:

Situation #1:
I was to meet a friend for a walk and she got stuck in traffic.

Proactive:
If my friend doesn't make it I will go for a walk anyways and enjoy the scenery. Maybe I will meet someone else or see someone I know on the path.

Reactive: Get upset that she was late or didn't make it a priority.

What I did: I found a new path that went down to a pretty creek.

In summary, being proactive involves taking initiative, planning ahead, and actively shaping one's destiny, while being reactive involves responding to events as they happen without necessarily having a long-term strategy or plan in place. By adopting a proactive mindset, individuals can exercise greater control over their lives and increase their chances of achieving desired outcomes.

When you're proactive, you're thinking ahead, planning for possibilities, showing up to open up, and building resilience.
Being proactive, you're shaping your life instead of letting it shape you.

Situation #2:
Someone gets a cut on their knee.

Proactive: Walk calmly to rinse, grab bandage, and care for it.

Reactive: Panic, yell, and scramble for help without a clear plan.

What happened: We cleaned it with a tissue and stopped the bleeding. Then put a bandage on it.

Being proactive can be as simple as planning what you'll do if a meeting runs long or a project hits a snag. I often write out possible scenarios and responses on a worksheet so I can reflect later on what really happened. It's a great learning tool—especially when working with others.

Practice here: What is a situation you can write in?

Situation #3:
_____.

Proactive Response: _____.

Reactive Response: _____
_____
_____.

What actually happened and how you handled it:_____
_____.

Situation #4:
_____.

Proactive Response: _____.

Reactive Response: _____
_____
_____.

What actually happened and how you handled it:_____
_____.

Summing it up on Proactive vs. Reactive Responses
When life throws something our way—whether it's a crooked picture frame, a frustrating comment, or an unexpected challenge—we usually have two options:

Reactive responses: immediate, emotional, often based on stress or old habits.

Proactive responses: thoughtful, intentional, based on what's best for us and others in the long run.

The key is noticing which one we're using. And that's where skills like executive functioning, memory, and energy management come in.

Executive Functioning: The Brain's CEO
Executive functioning is like the "CEO of the brain." It helps us plan, organize, sequence steps, notice how we're doing, and even imagine different choices. I saw this in action when I was substituting for a senior chair yoga class. The regular setup had all 25

students in rows, but many of them struggled to see where I was in the front. Instead of reacting with frustration or just keeping things the same, I paused, thought about the problem, and made a plan. We rearranged all the chairs into a big circle. Suddenly, everyone could see, and it made the class more fun and connected. I even offered options for different ability levels, and the students loved it.

That's executive functioning in real life: noticing, planning, sequencing, and then creating a better outcome.

Abstract Reasoning and Memory: Imagining Options and Remembering What Works

Abstract reasoning is what allows us to pause and ask and think, "what are my choices?" Memory helps us recall what worked before so we can do it again. Together, they shift us from reactive to proactive.

For example, after my traumatic brain injury and with aphasia, I've had to rethink how I use my energy. Because the brain is having to work harder with finding words or fixing the words I type in wrong, people with aphasia get fatigued a lot easier. So when I teach yoga or classes, I really focus on the preparation I need to be more present or if I have a lot going on before say I start a yoga class, I will show up a little early so I can pause, collect my thoughts, get the music going and the be present. Just showing up—teaching, being present with my kids, or even running errands—can take more willpower and focus than it did before. I've learned that my brain and body sometimes need a full afternoon nap, or even a "recovery day" after a big day out. Remembering to build rest into my schedule is part of being proactive. Instead of pushing myself until I get a migraine or get sick. My son is great at pointing this out to me and I really appreciate his awareness.

Attention and Processing: Focusing and Flow

Attention is the ability to focus on what matters. Processing is how quickly and accurately we can take in information and respond. Both are like muscles—they get stronger with practice, but they can also get tired if we're stressed, overworked, overwhelmed, worried and/or distracted.

Ski racing is a great example. Before a race, you slip the course, check your gear, fuel up with water, and focus on all the little details that set you up for success. That's attention at work—being intentional and prepared.

Then, when you're in the start gate, it's time to let go of things are not important right now, get focused on the starter and the area you are starting from so that when it is time to go, you can be focused in each turn, look ahead to what it coming and go with the flow. Processing takes over—you trust your training, your preparation, and your instincts.

But if you show up tired, stressed, or without your gear ready, everything gets harder. You risk injury, ski slower, and miss out on the fun. It's the same in daily life: when we focus our attention ahead of time, we can process better in the moment.

Energy: The Foundation of Proactive Choices

Our responses are directly tied to our energy. When we're well-rested, nourished, and calm, we can respond proactively. When we're exhausted, hungry, in pain, or stressed, it's much harder. Energy is impacted by so many things—sleep, mood, stress, nutrition, injuries, illness, even vision changes.

Managing energy became essential after my hysterectomy: Hot flashes, recovery pain, and fatigue made everything more draining. I found small adjustments that helped—like having my own blanket at night or scheduling breaks into my day. These changes gave me enough energy to lead with others around me.

Listening to the Body: Stress Signals
Sometimes our bodies tell us we're stressed before our minds catch up. Common signs of an overloaded nervous system include:
- Feeling like you need to escape (fight or flight).
- Racing heart or needing the bathroom.
- Yelling or being impatient.
- Craving sugary foods.
- Falling asleep even while sitting up.
- Wanting hugs or physical contact for comfort.

I've learned to see these not as "problems" but as signals—reminders that my nervous system needs support.

What are some of your Stress Signals? List them here...

Physiological Quieting: Calming the Nervous System
When those signals show up, we have choices. Instead of reacting from stress, we can practice "physiological quieting"—ways to calm the nervous system and restore balance:
- Drink something warm.
- Wrap up in a blanket.
- Walk outside or get out in nature.
- Move your body—run, stretch, or do yoga.
- Listen to calming or favorite music.
- Drink cold water.
- Close your eyes and meditate.
- Take deep breaths and become present.

What are some ways that you could help yourself find stillness, warmth or peace?

Putting It All Together
When we strengthen our executive functioning skills, set boundaries that work for us, lean in and implement simple techniques like GOAL or ACTION, and become more aware or have the ability to notice our energy, and listen to our body's signals, we give ourselves the power to pause. And in that pause, we can choose a proactive response instead of a reactive one.

That's where respect grows, communication improves, and connection deepens—whether in a yoga circle, in parenting, or in the everyday choices we make for ourselves. It is your ability to be proactive rather than reactive.

Sometimes these little concepts, change you in big ways. I'm going to leave space right here so you can come back and reflect or make notes on how being proactive can help you. What are some areas in your life right now that you would love to simply enjoy more or do with more ease?

Chapter 16

Make A Choice!

When it comes to decision-making, we all need a little help sometimes. Whether you're feeling tired or in a rush, this chapter is here to provide you with various ideas and references to aid you in making choices.

1. Folding It Down
Take a blank piece of paper and on one side write all your ideas - you can practice this with making a choice of what you will eat for your next meal. Maybe you want tacos, pizza, burgers, or a potato. You can write the word out or draw a picture. Then take the paper and fold the side with the ideas on it together in half. On the other side, pick a half of the page and narrow down from your ten ideas to five ideas. Then fold it again, and narrow it down again. If you would like, fold it down one more time and write the one final choice. There you have it! You made a choice for what you will eat. You can use this technique for any time you have a lot of ideas.

2. Rock Paper Scissors
You have to have another person to do this with unless you can find an app and challenge it. Do three strikes and the person who wins gets to do whatever it was that you were deciding on.

3. Count Down and Go
In slalom ski racing, the starter goes 5-4-3-2-1 and the racer can go on any number or after all the numbers are said. As a ski racing coach I encourage racers to pick the number they go on so that they aren't just waiting and trying to decide when to go.

4. Pomodoro™ Technique

Look it up online if you do not know this one. It is a technique for getting longer projects done. I have used it when writing books or completing projects that take a long time. What you do is work for 20 minutes and then take a ten minute break, then work again for 25 minutes and take a five minute break. And so on. For your break you want to walk away and do something completely different. You could go outside, go to the restroom, get a drink of water or take that ten minute nap.

5. Put on a Timer

This one is easy, but so often not used. Turn on a timer on your phone, watch, kitchen stove or whatever and stick to the time you set to get something done or work on a specific project for that amount of time. I use this to pull weeds because if I pull weeds for ten minutes each day it doesn't feel so overwhelming.

6. High Five in the Mirror

This is a Mel Robbins technique that allows you to acknowledge yourself when you walk by a mirror. How many of you actually do this? It can be a complete game changer for your self-c confidence as well as just noticing YOU. Try it. Now every time I go to the bathroom, I give myself a High-Five. At first it sounds funny and odd, but trust me it will help you so much!

7. Roll the Dice

Pick a number and roll the dice and see how close you are, or roll the dice and then that's how many push ups or whatever that you need to do. This can be really fun and help make a work out that once seemed impossible become I'm Possible.

8. Compare Pros and Cons
Take a piece of paper or a note on your phone and make comparison list of what is Pro or Good of a choice and what is Con or not so good of that choice. I use this on planning road trips or choosing places to eat dinner.

9. Goals
Write out or draw your goals on a piece of paper. If they are big goals refer to my GOAL chart to also write out where you are today, what could hold you back and what actions you can take that will allow you to jump over what's holding you back and closer to the goals that you set.

10. Smart Goals
Smart goals are ones that you know you can attain. Sometimes we have a big idea and we really just need to simplify them down into smaller smart goals.

11. Take ACTION
Use the paper to spell out the acronym, that way you can have an easier time getting it done.

12. Draw or map it out
Grab a piece of paper and some marker colors and begin to draw out your ideas or put your ideas on the paper and map out how they connect or what can be done together to save time. You could also use draw or map it out for what jobs you can give to someone else or cross out what isn't so important any longer.

13. Mind Mapping
There are apps and programs that can help you with mind mapping. You can look them up and then start mapping out all

that is on your mind. This will help you narrow down a way to get to where you need to be.

14. Start a Race
Sometimes putting your name in for a race, allows you to begin training for it. If you have a project, set the due date and then the steps to get there.

15. Add Fun to Get it Done
This one is my favorite. My good friend Mai would say turn up the music and we would dance our way through cleaning.

16. Make it a Puzzle
Doing the dishes is not my favorite chores, but when I add the ability to see how I can fit the dishes in the dishwasher like it is a puzzle, I get the job done.

17. Chunk it Together
Run errands in the same area of town. Choose to fold your laundry by type of clothes, colors or a persons laundry. Simplify what you need to do my setting out piles of paper or whatever it is. Take all the items out of your closet into another room, then only bring back what you really want or need.

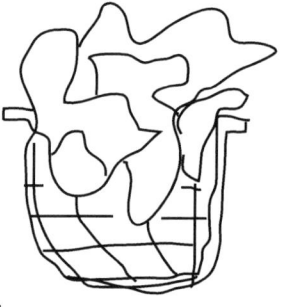

18. Create a Target of Importance
Draw a Target on your paper with a big circle then a smaller circle inside that, another one inside that, and one more. Then write what is most important target in the center, then the next, the next and the next.

19. Breathing exercises

Take your hands and place them at your heart center and notice your breath. Inhale and exhale just noticing how you are breathing. Is your breath long or shallow? Go ahead and take a deeper breath and notice the difference when you breathe in and out. You can even hold your breath and then slowly breathe out. There are many different breathing techniques that you can look up and use to help your focus and come into the present moment.

20. Draw a straw or paper answers

Take different lengths of paper and write answers on each one. Then line them up behind a desk or your hand so that they appear to be the exact same length at the top, allow another person to pick one.

21. Draw out a Funnel

I use this technique in business to take note of who I have contacted, what projects I am working on and what can become projects next. Draw a funnel like the drawing here and then write out next to it. It's good to do this on a dry-erase or chalk board as it is always getting updated.

Top of Funnel: Potential Work & Contacts

Middle Funnel: Proposals

Below the Funnel: Current Projects

22. Organize by Color

One day when I was substitute teaching in a class for a week, I realized all the students came in and found their notebooks based on the color of it. The notebooks were all just in a big pile.
I asked if we could organize by color and the teacher was excited and said YES. It worked so much better!

23. Musical chairs
Set up chairs in a circle with one less chair than the number of people you have in the group. Everyone lines up around the outside and music begins. Once the music stops everyone tries to sit on a chair, the person that doesn't have a chair is out. You then remove another chair and keep going down until there is one winner.

24. Don't decide
This one is easy… or is it?

25. Call on a good, positive and/or helpful friend
Ask someone else to help you decide or give their opinions on what you are trying to decide on. This can be fun when you are going shopping for a new outfit or shoes.

26. Turn to AI, like ChatGPT, or trusted research for help
We all have access to so much information so make sure that what you are basing your decision on is by a credible source. Universities and studies that involve more than 500 patrons is usually better to believe.

27. Put answers in a hat and draw one out
Got a hat? Got paper and a pen? Go for it. You can write out your choices and do this for yourself. Or maybe there is a group of you and you need to decide who presents first or goes first. Or maybe you have a lot of ideas and you want to choose which one to focus on.

28. Flip a coin - heads or tails?
Make sure you decide what answer is heads and what will be tails before you flip the coin in the air. And know that even if you

do not like what it landed on, that is a good indication that you want the other choice. When this is used in a soccer or sports game, realize if you win the flip choose the best for your team.

29. Ducks in a row - put in order to make a choice
You can write all your ideas out on paper or sticky notes and then put them in order to make a choice or follow the direction of what you need to do.

30. Drink Water.
If all else fails, go have a glass of water. Take a deep breathe and perhaps the answer will come to you.

Got any other ideas that have worked well for you? Use this space... to write more...

Choices Also Allow us to Create
Choices aren't just decisions—we use them to shape the rhythm of our days and the quality of our lives. Some choices guide us quickly, helping us move forward or simplify a moment. Others give us a chance to prepare, to pause, or to reset. Some choices open a doorway into creativity where we can explore without pressure.

When we allow ourselves the time and space to experiment, we discover new possibilities we never would have found in a hurry. Creativity grows when we're not rushing, judging, or expecting a polished result. The simple act of choosing to play, rest, or try something unfamiliar can shift our mood, expand our confidence, and remind us that life can feel lighter and more enjoyable when we give ourselves permission to explore.

Experimenting with choices invites us to create just for the joy of it. You might walk through a forest and gather fallen treasures—petals, leaves, twigs, grasses—and arrange them on the ground as if you're painting with nature. The design doesn't have to last; it's the experience of noticing, collecting, and creating that nourishes you. It's like you can leave a little treasure for the next person that comes along, but it doesn't have to be everywhere. They say that some hikers will tie clothing to trees to find there way up a path or know which way to go at a Y, yet in some National Parks guest went overboard with stacking rocks and so they have to advise people that there comes a time when it is art and a time when it is too much. So be mindful as you play with this concept of finding and leaving art. There is person near Bandon, Oregon who leaves patterns in the sand for people to enjoy until the ocean waves wash it away.

Another way to explore choice is through open-ended building. Give children (or adults!) a pile of blocks, legos, or other toys, and plenty of time, with no expectation of what should be built. Let their ideas unfold over hours or even days, allowing them to leave and return as inspiration shifts. When it's time to clean up, offer gentle notice rather than rushing the process—because sometimes the most meaningful creations are the ones that developed slowly, layer by layer, through curiosity and choice.

It's Our Choice
From exploring the many ways we can make a choice to recognizing that sometimes the choice is simply opening ourselves to what comes next, we reclaim our power. In every moment, big or small, we get to choose—and that freedom shapes how we live, grow, and experience our world.

Chapter 17
Functional Fitness & Movement

The "FUN" in functional is about finding joy in movements that not only build strength, balance and agility for daily living, yet also help us enjoy the activity. Some people think of fitness only as something we do if we are in shape. What about instead: be in shape with your movement and fitness every day.

Explore different kinds of fitness and activities and see what you like for this chapter or season of your life. Remember that your interests can change and sometimes finding a new practice or experience, opens you up to learning a way of being more fit and having more fun!

Think about how each one of these skills in good to be able to do. Here are ways to keep your body active, your mind sharp, and your heart engaged. You can try right at home (or almost anywhere) right now if you feel stable enough to do them. If you don't feel stable, find a counter, chair or friend you can lean on.

If you have health concerns, check in with a healthcare professional before starting something new. Movement is more than exercise—it's an invitation to play, grow, and challenge yourself.

Funictional Fitness for Real Life
It strengthens the muscles and movements you use every day—reaching, carrying, bending, and balancing—so tasks feel easier and safer. By building stability and mobility in natural movement patterns, you reduce strain, prevent injuries, and move with more confidence in every environment.

- **Lifting Boxes:** Use household items or boxes (with safe lifting technique where you pick up the box using your legs, core strength and arms) to strengthen your legs, arms, and core.
- **Climbing Stairs:** Each step is like training for a mountain adventure. Going up and down builds endurance, leg strength, and cardiovascular health.
- **Pull-Ups (or Rows):** If you've got a pull-up bar or sturdy chair, practice using your hands to pull yourself up. Think of it as building superhero strength for opening doors, carrying bags, or giving big hugs.
- **Jumping Jacks, Jumping Rope or Bunny Hops:** Shake out stress, boost your heart rate, and feel like a kid again! All are great for energy and coordination.
- **Push-Ups:** Channel your inner warrior. Whether on the floor, counter top, or wall, push-ups strengthen your arms, chest, and core for lifting, reaching, and hugging.
- **Squats:** Practice sitting and standing strong—like you're lowering onto your favorite comfy chair and then back up with energy.
- **Lunges:** Step into strength with lunges. They prepare your legs for walking, climbing stairs, or keeping up with friends/pets/kids/grandkids.
- **Planks:** Become a solid "bridge." Planks build core stability, which supports your back, posture, and balance.
- **Step-Ups:** Use a stair or sturdy surface to practice stepping up with confidence. Imagine climbing toward your next adventure.
- **Bicycle Crunches:** Lie back and pedal like you're riding toward joy. These fire up your core while moving your body in a playful rhythm.

The key to thriving isn't just one thing—it's the synergy of movement, recovery, and nourishment. When these elements work together, your body and mind feel stronger, more resilient, and more joyful.

By combining these three pillars, you create a foundation that not only strengthens your body but also nurtures your mind and spirit. Movement becomes more fun, recovery more effective, and daily life more vibrant.

Focus on these three pillars:

Pillar I: Move with awareness: Whether it's yoga, functional fitness, or team sports, pay attention to your body, your breath, and the joy of motion.

Pillar II: Recover intentionally: Use tools like cold plunges, steam, the REST method, and restorative sleep to give your body the time it needs to heal and restore energy.

Pillar III: Fuel your body well: Support your movement and recovery with nutrient-rich foods, hydration, and the vitamins and minerals your body needs to thrive.

Your body is your greatest ally—treat it with intention, care, and a little playfulness, and it will respond with energy, resilience, and joy.

When we honor ourselves, we can choose fitness and movement that keeps us feeling good. There are a variety of ways to integrate fitness in for you. I believe that Yoga is a wonderful form of exercise, stretching and mindfulness practice that can help build sustainability in our mindset and body wellness.

Here are important aspects to consider for overall functional fitness and movement:

Agility: Agility refers to the ability to change direction quickly, move with precision, and maintain control of your body during physical activities. Developing agility improves your coordination, reaction time, and performance in sports and daily living. Strength: Building strength involves increasing muscle mass and enhancing the ability of your muscles to exert force. Strength training exercises, such as lifting weights or bodyweight exercises, help to improve muscle tone, enhance bone density, and support joint stability. Strong muscles are important for overall functional fitness and can help prevent injuries.

Endurance/Stamina: Endurance or stamina is the ability to sustain prolonged physical activity without getting excessively tired. It is crucial for activities like running, cycling, swimming, or participating in endurance sports. Endurance training improves cardiovascular health, boosts energy levels, and enhances the efficiency of your body's oxygen utilization.

Balance: Balance refers to the ability to maintain stability and control over your body's position. It plays a vital role in preventing falls, especially as you age. Balance exercises, such as yoga or tai chi, can help improve core strength, posture, and coordination, reducing the risk of injuries and helping performance.

I have found there are a couple different ways to try to get in functional fitness. One is a well-rounded fitness routine that incorporates agility, strength, endurance, and balance training offers numerous benefits.

For this, you would create a daily work out schedule just like your work or appointment schedule. You will indicate what time your work outs are and choose a variety of ways to stay fit, for instance maybe you do

    Swimming Saturday
    Sleeping Sunday
    Movement with Music Monday
    Taking 10,000 Steps Tuesday
    Workout Wednesday
    Team Sport Thursday;
    FUNctional Fitness Friday

You can also design your work outs around the seasons: for instance in the winter it is ski race coaching and yoga. In the summer, I am kayaking and hiking, with yoga as my stretching component for the other activities.

Some people like to have daily goals where they get in 10,000 steps a day and do 50 sit ups each day along with other specific challenges.

Our bodies were designed to be active, they were not designed to just sit. The benefits of consistency in just moving and staying active are that you:

- Improve overall physical performance/function
- Enhance body composition in muscle mass and decreased body fat
- Increase bone density and reduced risk of osteoporosis
- Better cardiovascular health and lowered risk of chronic diseases
- Improve flexibility, mobility, and joint stability
- Increase energy levels and improved mood
- Reduce risk of injuries

Prioritizing movement can be one way that you can reduce your time on social media or scrolling through tiktok or whatever it is on your screen that is stealing your time away from what is good for you. Schedule time for fitness, then set down the phone and enjoy the silence as you get really focused, and begin.

Ready to try it?

Here's a simple concept to start...

Daily Movement: Steps, Stamina, and Staying Active
Movement doesn't have to be complicated or take hours at the gym.

One simple goal that has big benefits is aiming for around 10,000 steps a day of walking:
- Improves cardiovascular endurance
- Strengthens muscles in the legs and core
- Supports joint health
- Boosts mood, creativity, and mental clarity
- Gives you a natural rhythm for your day

How could you increase your steps throughout your day?
1. Park farther from the store?
2. Take a short walking break?
3. Walk with a friend after a meal?
4. Get up an dance?
5. Attend a yoga or fitness class today?

One of the best lessons I've learned coaching youth soccer is how much fun warm-ups and cool-downs can be when athletes are invited to design them. Younger players follow instructions, but as kids grow, giving them space to create their own routines builds ownership, excitement, and teamwork. It also reinforces that moving safely and intentionally can be playful and creative—just like all these functional fitness ideas.

As I live my life with intentional breathing integrated in that I have learned through playing the oboe as a child and then doing yoga, I've noticed can even be integrated on a soccer field, ski hill, or other fitness activities. I have noticed that I am able to catch my breath easier after a quick sprint and I can intentionally notice my breath as I am moving forward, and I can pause to take it all in and enjoy the view or even the moments on the side line. I challenge you to bring breath awareness into activities.

Breathing and Pause Focus
- Notice your inhale. Notice your exhale.
- Right now, notice where your feet are on the floor/ground.
- Raise your hands up towards the sky then bring your hands back to your heart. And pause.
- Bring your shoulders down and back. Lead with your heart center forward.
- Notice your inhale. Notice your exhale.
- Come back to your heart and just send a little extra love and attention to you.
- Enjoy this moment to just pause.
- Maybe look around where you are and connect with what is around you.
- Smile.

Just taking a moment to pause, even when reading all of this, or going out into the world to experience all it has to offer, is a gift in itself. Just pause. Enjoy the moment. Maybe even bring your hands to your heart and send a little extra gratitude to you!

Here are some ideas of Group, Individual and Team Fitness below. Maybe you can circle ones you have done or make notes next to what you would like to try this year, next or...

Try a Group Fitness Class:
- HIIT (High-Intensity Interval Training): Fast bursts of activity with short recovery periods—perfect for boosting cardio and endurance in a playful, energizing way.
- Spinning/Cycling: Simulate an outdoor ride indoors; great for heart health, leg strength, and racing toward your goals (with out falling off the bike!).
- Zumba: Dance like nobody's watching. Latin and international beats get your body moving while your spirit smiles.
- Barre: Ballet-inspired movements mixed with Pilates and strength training—sculpt, tone, and lengthen muscles while feeling graceful.
- Bootcamp: Full-body workouts with a mix of cardio, strength, and endurance. Imagine yourself training like a superhero.
- Pilates: Low-impact and focused on core strength, flexibility, and alignment. Using precise movements and controlled breathing, Pilates improves posture, muscle tone, and body awareness.
- Yoga: Flexibility, strength, and calm all in one. Yoga classes at gyms provide a range of styles—gentle, dynamic, or some where in between.
- Strength Training: Build power with weights, resistance bands, or bodyweight exercises. Strong muscles make daily life easier and more fun.
- Aqua Fitness: Low-impact aerobic workouts in water—great for joints and adding a playful splash to your routine.

Martial Arts
- Karate: Strikes, kicks, and blocks with a focus on self-defense, discipline, and mental focus.
- Taekwondo: High and spinning kicks, fast movements, and patterns that build speed and agility.
- Brazilian Jiu-Jitsu: Ground-based grappling and submission techniques—strategy and leverage over brute strength.
- Muay Thai: The "Art of Eight Limbs" from Thailand, combining punches, kicks, elbows, and knees.
- Kung Fu: Wide-ranging Chinese martial arts incorporating strikes, kicks, acrobatics, and traditional routines.

Individual Sports
- Walking/Hiking : Enjoy this on your own, with your dog, with friends or find a walking/hiking group to join in your area!
- Road or Trail Running: Try different routes or go the same way; register for fun races and events in order to help you set goals and achieve them. Agility, strength and endurance.
- Horseback Riding or Competitive Riding: Got a horse? What a great way to care for an animal and get to adventure with it, too.
- Biking - Electric, Mountain or Road: Often biking gives you the ability to travel at various speeds, distances and routes Excellent fitness choice for building muscles and endurance.
- Swimming: Find a pool, a team, or go open water swimming with a wet suit or life jacket and buoy. Great for endurance, strength and building up your cardiovascular strength.
- Scuba Diving: What a beautiful world it is under the water! Excellent for cardiovascular strength, peaceful for mind.
- Water-skiing or Wake-boarding: Great for strength, agility.
- Skiing - downhill/cross country: Full body endurance, stamina, strength, resiliency, agility and balance. Great views, too!

Team Sports
- Soccer (Football): Builds cardiovascular fitness, agility, coordination, and teamwork.
- Basketball: Agility, endurance, teamwork in a fast-paced game.
- Baseball/Softball: Hand-eye coordination, throwing, catching, and working together as a team.
- Volleyball: Jump, dive, spike—great for upper body strength, teamwork, and fun competition.
- American Football/Rugby/Rugby Sevens: Strength, strategy, and endurance in high-energy, team-focused sports.
- Tennis/Badminton/Table Tennis/Pickle ball: Quick reflexes, hand-eye coordination, and cardio—play solo or doubles.
- Golf: Precision, focus, and low-impact movement that still gets you outside.
- Ice Hockey/Field Hockey/Lacrosse: Stick handling, running, and teamwork. A great way to challenge agility/coordination.
- Handball: Fast-paced, combining elements of basketball, soccer, and hockey.
- Water Polo: Swimming, passing, and teamwork in a water-based challenge.
- Wheelchair Soccer or Basketball: Passing, shooting, and strategic movement—great for teamwork, strength and focus.
- Ultimate Frisbee: Throw, catch, run, and collaborate in a non-contact, high-energy game out in nature.
- Pickle ball: Fun, fast, and social, improving hand-eye coordination and cardio fitness.

Bringing It All Together for Your Health & Wellbeing
Functional fitness isn't just for the gym—it's a way of living. You can integrate it into your daily routines, your travel adventures, and even your business meetings. Sitting at a desk all day doesn't have to define your work life; standing up to stretch,

walking during phone calls, taking the stairs, or adding small movement breaks can shift your energy and sharpen your focus.

Traveling With Movement in Mind
Travel naturally invites us to step out of routine—and that includes how we move. Whether we're visiting a theme park, heading to the beach, or exploring another country, our bodies and brains thrive when we gently weave fitness into the experience. It doesn't need to feel like "working out" at all. In fact, some of the best movement happens when you're simply enjoying the moment, exploring a new place, or staying curious about what your body can do.

One of the most surprising places to practice functional fitness is a theme park like Disneyland. You can easily walk twenty to thirty thousand steps a day without even realizing it. A little planning makes the experience much more enjoyable: wearing supportive shoes, carrying a small backpack, packing a water bottle, and choosing clothing that lets you move freely. Snacks—brought from home or purchased there—keep your energy up so you don't hit the late-afternoon slump. Breaks matter, too. Pausing to watch a parade becomes an opportunity to stretch your calves, roll your shoulders, or take a few deep breaths. Even bathroom lines can turn into quick mobility moments. And if you're standing in line with kids, playful stretches or even a short dance while the music plays makes the wait feel fun rather than tiring.

A simple weekend at the beach offers a completely different kind of movement—grounded, rhythmic, and often harder than it looks. Walking on sand strengthens your feet, ankles, and stabilizing muscles in ways a treadmill can't match. You can turn the outing into an adventure by rock-hounding, walking long stretches of shoreline, or jumping in the waves if the conditions are safe. Swimming in the ocean works your whole body and gives your mind a refreshing reset. For those who enjoy trying new activities, beach towns often offer kayaking, paddleboarding, surfing lessons, fishing, or crabbing off a pier. Even wandering through local museums, aquariums, or tiny coastal shops keeps you moving in a gentle, enjoyable way. You don't have to turn every trip into an athletic event—just choosing options that invite motion gives your body what it needs.

International travel introduces movement opportunities you may never have at home. Cities and small towns often encourage walking or biking as part of everyday life, which makes it easy to join in. Instead of racing from destination to destination, slowing down lets you truly take in the culture—meeting locals, exploring side streets, and noticing the textures, colors, and rhythms of a place. Many travelers enjoy golfing in other countries, using it as a calming way to see new landscapes while staying active. Depending on where you're visiting, you may be able to try activities that aren't common in your area—cricket, spearfishing, yoga styles unique to the region, or other sports rooted in local tradition. These experiences blend learning, movement, and cultural connection in a way that stays with you forever.

Your body is designed to move. Your organs, blood flow, oxygen exchange, and cellular activity all thrive when you're adjusting, stretching, changing positions, and opening yourself to what's next. Movement keeps you alive, alert, and resilient. The more you honor that natural design, the better you feel—in every part of your life.

I have developed an app that can be found at www.HealthyFunChoices.com. It offers creative ideas around fitness, foods, time management, encouragement and so much more. I hope you can find it or find what is next!

Chapter 18

Healing & Self-Care

Resiliency isn't about pretending everything is fine. It's the ability to bend without breaking — to adapt, breathe, and stay connected to your inner strength even when circumstances change. A positive attitude adds a gentle, steady light to that strength. Together, they shape the way we heal, cope, and grow through injury, illness, or disability.

We often imagine recovery as a return—a path that circles us back to who we once were. But real healing rarely works that way. We don't rewind. We don't rebuild a replica of our old selves. Instead, we grow into someone new, shaped by what we have learned, what we've endured, and what we now understand about strength, adaptability, and our own capacity for courage. Healing becomes a process of becoming, not returning.

Athletes who have faced life-changing injuries often speak to this truth. In Full Circle, Trevor Kennison shares how his accident didn't end his life as an athlete — it radically transformed it. He learned to redefine freedom, performance, and identity in his sit-ski, discovering new lines, new terrain, and a new version of himself that he never expected. His message is powerful: the "new you" is not a lesser version — it's simply different, and in many ways, more expansive than before.

Kevin Pearce, co-founder of Love Your Brain, echoes a similar message after his traumatic brain injury. He often talks about how life didn't go "back to normal" after his crash. Instead, he found a deeper purpose in connection, mindfulness, and service. His journey shows that healing can open doors we never would have sought out—doors into compassion, presence, and community that only hardship can reveal. This is what becoming new looks like: honoring where you came from while embracing what your experience allows you to offer now.

Tony Drees, a Paralympian and veteran who survived catastrophic injuries, often speaks about "choosing to rise"—not by pretending things are easy, but by refusing to let pain or disability erase possibility. He teaches that growth is not about regaining what was lost; it's about exploring what is now possible. His story reminds us that resilience is less about bouncing back and more about expanding forward, becoming wiser, braver, and more intentional with every step.

In the Aphasia Recovery Connection community, thousands of people connect online and in workshops thanks to the founders' vision of bringing individuals with aphasia together. Their shared stories show that life after stroke or brain injury doesn't go back to what it was—it grows forward. ARC members often say recovery isn't about getting your old words back, but discovering new ways to communicate, new confidence, and new strength in each small step. Their experiences remind us that healing is measured not just in speech, but in resilience, support, and the courage to keep showing up. Personally, I was lucky to find ARC on Facebook because it gave me an ability to share messages, speak up and realize that we all need to speak up more about Aphasia.

Aphasia is a communication difference that affects how a person understands, speaks, reads, or writes. It doesn't change intelligence—it simply changes how language moves in and out of the brain. Every person has a different aphasia experience and diagnosis. In fact, many doctors and therapists have troubles diagnosing exactly what it might be because language is hard to understand especially when the patient can't quite explain what it is that isn't working like it used to. Many people with aphasia find that familiar tasks still make perfect sense, while new information or multi-step directions can feel tangled or confusing. Support tools make an enormous difference. I use AI to help me write clearly, check what I understand, or break instructions into step-by-step pieces. Speech-to-text lets me record my thoughts when typing is difficult, and automatic spell check helps clean up the words that come out jumbled. These tools don't replace my voice—they give me pathways to express it, stay independent, and feel confident as I continue to learn, grow, and communicate in my own way. What you are reading here is absolutely written by me over years and years of writing collections and workshop presentations bringing everything together. Just like at the very beginning of this book I had to live it first.

Your Mindset Directly Affects Your Body

The brain and body communicate constantly. When we practice hope, curiosity, gratitude, or self-compassion, our nervous system softens and settles. This lowers stress hormones, improves sleep, supports immune function, and allows our body to repair itself more efficiently. It's not about forced positivity — it's about creating a calmer internal environment where healing feels safe.

Healing is rarely linear or one-way. There are flare-ups, setbacks, and discouraging days. Resiliency reminds you:

Today is one chapter, not the whole story.

I can try again tomorrow.

I can find another way.

People with strong resiliency stay more engaged in their self-care routines, show up more consistently for physical therapy or movement practices, and are more likely to ask for help or use tools that support them.

Research shows that when people practice optimism, mindfulness, or intentional reframing, pain often feels less overwhelming and recovery feels more possible. Challenges become less personal and more like something to work with rather than something happening to you. As your mindset softens, the body follows—muscles stop guarding, the nervous system relaxes, and the mind becomes more open to solutions and healing.

A resilient, positive mindset makes space for self-care to become flexible and uplifting. You may find yourself trying gentle movements, adjusting routines without guilt, exploring new hobbies or therapies, or letting nature, creativity, or breath work support your healing. Small wins feel easier to celebrate, and even when mobility or energy shifts, self-care can stay aligned with your needs and who you are in the moment.

Whether recovering from surgery, navigating aphasia, living with chronic illness, or adapting to a disability, every small effort—a stretch, a walk, a deep breath, or a kind word to yourself—reinforces your belief in your ability to heal and adapt. Over time, these small acts create a strong inner trust: "I am capable. I can face this."

Resiliency and positivity help you move from passively waiting for healing to actively participating in it. You support your body by choosing nourishing foods, drinking water, practicing safe movement, spending time outside, seeking community, using helpful tools and supports like breath work or speech-to-text, and resting intentionally. These choices signal to your body that you are working with it, making healing more effective and empowering.

Healing becomes something you do with your body, not something you passively hope for. Healing is an active process that includes your mindset and fully committing to sending loving thoughts to healing that spot or tender area. It involves doing the activities or physical therapy or icing that is required to get it to be better. And, it includes intentionally sleeping, taking naps and pausing so you can rest.

Many people think that when you have pain, you have to completely stop everything you are doing and sit on the couch or chair until the pain goes away. Pain is not to stop you, rather it is to get your attention. Pain can be a warning sign, yes, but there are so many serious health conditions that come forward and show no signs of pain. So please do not just think you are supposed to stop and do nothing because you have pain.

Personally, I live with pain every single day. I do activities to keep me busy and not to think about my pains because there is an active life that I choose to live.

Maintaining a positive attitude during physical therapy or any healing-focused treatment doesn't mean ignoring the discomfort — it means showing up with openness, patience, and belief in your ability to improve. A hopeful mindset helps you stay engaged, reduces fear, and allows your body to relax into new movements. When you approach each session with curiosity instead of frustration, you create the inner conditions that make progress easier and more sustainable. Even small improvements feel more meaningful when you let yourself celebrate them.

Therapy works best when it continues beyond the appointment. The exercises and practices your provider gives you to do at home are essential because they retrain your muscles, nervous system, and brain through repetition and consistency. Doing the work only once a week isn't enough—healing happens in the small daily actions and the gentle reminders your body receives over time. Practicing at home, asking for help when you need it, and making these exercises part of your routine will help you recover faster, strengthen your confidence, and feel more in control of your progress.

The Healthy & Fun Choices Way is meant to live a life that you want to live. Your body tells you when it needs a pause, and listening can prevent injury, speed healing, and even make movement more enjoyable.

Here are ways that can offer wake up to your body that might be trying to get your attention:
- Cold Plunges: Reduce inflammation, improve circulation, and wake up your nervous system.
- Steam Showers/Saunas: Relax muscles, support detoxification through sweat, and calm the mind.
- Rest & Relaxation: Raise your limb, ice/heat as doctor recommends.

When injuries do happen, many have found The REST Method helps. Injuries happen, even to the most careful athletes.

A helpful guideline is the REST method:
- R – Rest: Give the injured area time to heal.
- E – Elevate: Raise the injured limb above heart level to reduce swelling.
- S – Support: Use wraps, braces, or compression to protect the area while it is healing (listen to your doctor).
- T – Treat: Ice, heat, or other therapeutic interventions as appropriate.

Did you know that icing the back of your knees can help reduce inflammation in other areas of your body? I learned this when my right leg was in a bad way, they call it "opposite syndrome effect," meaning work done on one leg—like ice, heat, or even acupuncture—can help the other leg as well. My leg had nine surgeries and a stubborn wound wouldn't heal. Direct work on that leg wasn't possible, but my acupuncturist could treat the other leg—and amazingly, it helped reduce swelling and support healing in the injured leg. It's a perfect example of how the body is interconnected, and how creative recovery strategies can make a real difference.

Physical Therapy and When It Is Important:
Physical therapy is a specialized form of rehabilitation that focuses on restoring and improving physical function, reducing pain, and enhancing mobility. It is often recommended when recovering from injuries, surgeries, or certain medical conditions that affect movement and function. Physical therapy can help:
- Recover from orthopedic injuries: fractures, sprains/strains
- Rehabilitate after surgeries, joint replacements
- Manage chronic pain and improve mobility
- Restore movement and function after a stroke or TBI
- Address balance, flexibility and strength

Physical therapists are trained professionals who assess your specific needs, develop customized treatment plans, and guide you through exercises and therapies to optimize your physical health and recovery. If you experience any limitations, pain, or difficulties with physical function, consulting with a physical therapist can be beneficial in addressing your unique needs and improving your overall physical fitness.

Lower or Upper Back:
Back issues can be categorized into lower back pain (lumbar region) or upper back pain (thoracic region). Lower back pain is more common and often attributed to muscle strain, poor posture, or spinal conditions like herniated discs. Upper back pain is usually associated with muscle tension, poor posture, or underlying conditions affecting the thoracic spine.

Treatment for back issues may involve a combination of rest, pain management, physical therapy, and lifestyle modifications. It is essential to consult with a healthcare professional to determine the underlying cause and appropriate treatment options for your specific condition.

Be intentional in how you get in and out of bed at night and in the morning. I believe a lot of our back issues happen when we sleep. We toss and turn without having too much knowledge of how we are doing it. Here are some intentional movements that might help you more:
- Position and rotate your knees and feet together
- Engage your core stomach when you turn over
- Think about how you turn over
- Sleeping on your side, bend your knees slightly
- Adjust often so you don't get stuck all twisted

Add stretching, yoga and functional fitness to your every day to help live with more ease and joy. Practicing good posture consistently throughout the day is essential for long-term benefits. Be mindful of your posture not only while sitting but also during other activities like standing, walking, and lifting objects.

Maintaining good posture is crucial for preventing and managing back issues. Here are some tips to improve posture:
- Sit up straight: Sit with your back against the chair, shoulders relaxed, and spine aligned. Avoid slouching.

- Engage your core: Strengthening your core muscles can provide support to your spine and improve posture.
- Practice pulling your belly button in toward your spine with a straight back.
- Keep shoulders down and back: Avoid rounding your shoulders forward. Roll your shoulders down and back, opening up your chest and aligning your upper back.
- Use ergonomic support and add supportive cushions to maintain proper spinal alignment while sitting.
- Take regular breaks: Avoid sitting for prolonged periods. Get up, stretch, and walk around at regular intervals to relieve muscle tension and promote blood circulation.
- Use proper lifting techniques: When lifting heavy objects, use your legs rather than your back, and avoid twisting.
- Wear good shoes that have insoles or orthotics.

Incorporate exercises that target back and core muscles, such as back extensions, planks, and rows, to strengthen the muscles supporting your spine.

Maintain a healthy weight to help your posture, remember that excess weight can strain the back. Engaging in regular exercise and maintaining a healthy weight can alleviate stress on the spine. Ensure your desk, chair, and computer are set up ergonomically to promote good posture. Position the screen at eye level, adjust the chair height, and use a supportive chair with proper lumbar support.

If you experience persistent or severe back issues, consider consulting with a physical therapist or chiropractor. They can provide specific exercises, therapies, or adjustments to address your posture and alleviate pain.

Chapter 19

Yoga is Magic

Yoga has taught me that movement is about more than stretching and strengthening muscles—it's about living with more awareness and ease.

Yoga is often seen as a workout as a series of poses—but at its heart, yoga is a way of being. It's about how we carry ourselves, how we breathe, and how we meet life's challenges with greater presence. Incorporating these principles into daily life—not just on a mat—can help us live with more balance, kindness, and awareness.

Yoga is Excellent for All Ages & Abilities
I first discovered yoga in college, during a time when I was struggling with constant pain from endometriosis. A friend suggested I try a yoga class for PE credit, and I was hesitant, but curious. That class changed my life. My instructor helped me find poses that gently stretched my body and eased the pain I felt in my core and lower back. More importantly, I learned how to slow my breath—something that gave me comfort and relief when nothing else seemed to help. Yoga became a Godsend.

After college, yoga continued to weave its way into my life. I practiced at home, attended classes twice a week, and learned from a variety of teachers. One teacher pushed us to move outside our comfort zones into challenging poses. That was perfect for me in my twenties—when energy and curiosity made it fun to test my limits. Today, though, my practice looks very different. I no longer measure yoga by headstands or one-armed balances. Instead, it's about listening to my body and honoring what it needs. If today my knee would appreciate extra support, I bring a knee cushion. If I am feeling really strong, maybe I add in more mini cobras or hold down dog longer or stand like a pencil for five minutes with my inhale and exhales as my arms are reached high to the sky, my core pulled in and my feet firmly planted on the ground.

Over my three decades of doing yoga as a regular practice and teaching it for the last five years, I have experienced many different styles of yoga. In fact, trying different styles and teachers is important because you can gain something new from each. One teacher introduced music and chanting, creating a space that felt deeply spiritual. Another time, I fell in love with Bikram hot yoga. The sequence was always the same, and my body learned to flow with it almost in a trance. By the end, I was drenched in sweat—sometimes I'd step right into the shower with my clothes still on, then toss them in the washer. That season of yoga was intense, transformative, and exactly what I needed at the time.

But everything shifted in 2017, after my first major car accident. With a traumatic brain injury and ongoing dizziness, hot yoga was no longer possible. I couldn't complete my yoga teacher training, and suddenly the practice I loved had to change completely. Yoga became less about pushing myself and more about simply standing without support or sitting without nausea.

Lean in & Learn through the Practice of Practicing
Through all of these changes, yoga has continued to be my teacher. It reminds me that how I carry myself—even in hardship—matters. Yoga philosophy helps guide me, especially the Yamas and Niyamas, two of its core teachings have allowed me to understand a broader base for yoga. I don't have to be upset at myself for not being able to do what others can do. I can let go of what no longer serves me in my practice and my daily life. I can also lean into what feels truthful and content.

There are other advantages of Yoga that come from our ways of thinking and responding. Yamas are ethical principles to live by with intention. They include non-violence, truthfulness, non-stealing, moderation, and non-possessiveness. Niyamas are personal observances that we strive for bringing in as practices to the studio, our homes and the way we live. They include cleanliness, contentment, self-discipline, self-study, and surrendering to something greater than ourselves.

Yoga Benefits You Beyond the Yoga Mat
These principles extend far beyond the yoga mat. They remind us that yoga is not only about what we do—it's about who we become.

Yoga class usually includes a series of yoga poses that are presented by the teacher who talks you through your inhales and exhales while you move into a series of poses. A typical yoga practice often includes a series of poses, starting with a warm-up and ending with a cool-down. The warm-up usually involves gentle movements, stretches, and breathing exercises to prepare the body and mind for the practice ahead. It may include poses like Cat-Cow, Child's Pose, and Sun Salutations.

In the middle of the class, your teacher might have you go through a series of poses and add on other poses to keep the practice unique and not mundane. Or you may find a teacher that likes to do a similar class each time so your body is able to connect with the familiar and then deepen your experience. Neither one way or the other is better in my opinion, but I definitely appreciate teachers who say the inhale and exhale along with the movement as it really allows our breath work to expand our movements and get the attention of our brain.

Enjoy It All

If you have any questions around yoga, simply reach out or ask a yoga teacher. We can help you further your practice or send you to some good books and videos, too. There are several styles of yoga, each emphasizing different aspects of the practice:

Vinyasa Flow Yoga: A dynamic style of yoga that synchronizes movement with breath, often in a continuous flow.

Balance Yoga: Focuses on developing stability, coordination, and mental focus through various balancing poses.

Strength Yoga: A practice that aims to build strength, tone muscles, and improve overall physical fitness through yoga poses.

Core Yoga: Specifically targets the core muscles, aiming to strengthen and stabilize the abdominal and back muscles.

Yin Yoga: A slow-paced practice that involves holding passive poses for an extended period, targeting deep connective tissues.

Restorative Yoga: Utilizes props to support the body in relaxing poses, promoting deep relaxation and rejuvenation.

Hot Yoga: Practiced in a heated room, typically around 95-105°F (35-40°C), deeper stretching and increases detoxification.

Sound Bath Yoga: Combines traditional yoga poses with sound healing, using instruments like singing bowls or gongs to enhance relaxation and meditation.

Chapter 20

Just Show Up to Open Up

A couple of years ago, I attended a leadership conference and had an interesting and unforgettable encounter at the airport. While purchasing water and a magazine, I struck up a conversation with a woman wearing beautiful feather earrings that complemented her outfit.

As I prepared for the conference, I had to be mindful of my recovery from accidents that occurred a year and a half earlier. Taking into consideration my neck and back issues, I worked with my doctors, speech therapists, and physical therapists to ensure a comfortable journey. I packed light, brought a neck pillow and walking sticks for stability, and opted for a rolling suitcase instead of a backpack to minimize strain.

I boarded my airplane and found my seat, relieved that it was on the right side, which was more comfortable for my neck. To my surprise, the lady with the earrings ended up sitting next to me! We laughed and started chatting. She revealed that she was a shamanic healer specializing in shoulder, back, and neck pain.

I thought what are the chances? Right place, right time. After I explained my challenges, she offered to provide healing during the flight, and I agreed. Though I didn't feel anything physically, I focused on accepting her healing energies and engaged in meaningful conversation. We even exchanged phone numbers and planned to meet for lunch the next day.

Upon arriving at the conference, I joined my roommate and began navigating the bustling environment. To accommodate my needs, I strategically chose a spot in the middle of the conference room, avoiding excessive head movements. Coincidentally, the healer from the plane sat next to me once again, and we both marveled at the synchronicity. We chatted about how her healing may have contributed to my improved tolerance of the loud music at the event.

Throughout the conference, I used creative strategies to manage my traumatic brain injury (TBI) and enhance my experience. I took photos with new acquaintances to aid my memory, as face-name recognition was challenging for me. These photos served as a way to exchange contact information, ensuring I could connect with them later. This concept worked so well, that still to this day, five years later, I still take photos when I meet someone new and send them my contact info through the text with the photo of us.

I discovered quiet areas, like a cozy bathroom with soft chairs, and an outdoor space, to retreat when the sensory stimuli became overwhelming. I also relied on mints to calm my nervous system and identified a seating area away from the flashing lights.

During breaks, I proactively engaged with other attendees, including headline speakers' and familiar faces from professional associations. Despite the hectic environment, I made connections that would later lead to valuable client relationships.

The conference provided the inspiration and momentum for my subsequent pivot in response to the pandemic-induced job loss and fueled my business with work for the next couple of years.

Throughout my conference experience, I noticed that as I brought in The Healthy & Fun Choices Way, I learned the importance of infusing fun into activities and interactions.

Here are some creative and enjoyable approaches you can use, too, to remember names:
- Take a photo with the person and exchange contact information via text message.
- Engage in a handshake while repeating the person's name and asking them to repeat yours.
- Go around in a circle, stating each person's name, preferred pronouns, and using a word that starts with the same letter as their name (e.g., Kind Kirsten, Cool Cody, Dangerous Dane, Kool Kaia).
- Create a memorable jingle or rhyme associated with the person's name.
- Identify your name with a color or animal as you say your name and then repeat them to remember.

Another time I realized how just showing up can help you open up is when I applied and won a scholarship to attend a Love Your Brain Retreat in Colorado in 2023. When I was in the airport and found other people attending the retreat, I realized we all shared a similar challenge of not being able to remember names. So instead of just skipping it, I started talking more with them to figure out images or rhymes or other ways that we could remember each others' names. I often point to my ears and then hold up the number ten with my hands to indicate K- "ears" - ten. Another friend I met, we came up with the sun-ray motion with our hands to remember Ray. Then this one guy was super funny and he quickly says just remember me like "Doormat" for Matt. As you can see I still know their names even after a few years!

Sometimes I will let them know about TBI and Aphasia. Did you know you can also wear a sunflower lanyard when you are in airports or other locations to let people know you have a hidden disability.

Just ask.
Just be who you are in the moment and smile. People like to feel connected, so asking and carrying on conversations is important to being seen, heard and understood.
Sometimes asking more questions about where they live or what they like to do can help in remembering.

This ability to speak up or show up, even when you don't know someone is a skill and an important one to have. I encourage you to practice at home, in the shower or a mirror; and then just try it a get together or event.

Being able to carry on a conversation with others is a very important skill to have, brain injury or not, regardless of your age by showing that you care and are willing to ask questions and listen can go a long way. Good conversation starter ideas:

- Mention that you like their music or that you don't
- Point out a bird that you see or tree in the distance
- Compliment them on something like their eyes
- Ask about their pet or the activity you both doing
- Find out what town or area they live in

Here is a funny story that happened because I said hello to someone while hiking on a hot summer day in Central Oregon. I found out the guy noticed the logo on my daughters shirt. It happened to be one of the first logos that I designed as a graphic designer in college. He said that he had seen that Orthodontist when he was a teen and that he still loves his smile! I said "well, that's funny because my dad, your orthodontist, is right behind me coming down the hill!" The two got to chat and have a great conversation.

Another time I met two women sitting in a creek who actually grew up in the same home town I did. Recently I saw a solid kayak that was similar to a paddle board, upon asking the man about it, I discovered that he was a metal fab designer which is an industry that my son is interested in. All our similarities provide connection. How will you show up today?

Being Vulnerable
Showing up—truly showing up—is about more than physically being in a space or a room. It's about bringing your whole self, your attention, and your intention into the moment, even when you're navigating fear, uncertainty, or past challenges.

For three years I took an online course by Mel Robbins called Launch! Each time we picked projects or topics we wanted to launch, one year it was about launching ourselves. We all got to know Mel on a personal basis and over that time period she was using our meetings as a way to learn and get feedback on what she was creating. She shared the idea that people will always have opinions, judgments, or comments. Her advice? Let them. Let people have their thoughts. They don't define you, and they don't need to shape your choices.

This was life-changing for me because all the comments and criticisms I experienced, I could just let them. When I stopped worrying about invisible critics and focused on my purpose, I was able to enjoy life and connect with people more easily. The last launch I got to the very end of it and got really frustrated because I realized how much time and energy I had given everyone else than my own goals, dreams, books, courses and classes. I had to let it go and realize there is no specific due date.

The first year was a small group, and I discovered how powerful it is to open up and share vulnerabilities—about my accidents, my divorce, and other life challenges. I started to find my voice and my willingness to be seen and build trust. I still have friends from the program. This practice reinforced a central truth for me: showing up is a choice, and a way to live.

In the context of showing up: focus on what you want to bring and accomplish, rather than what could go wrong. When I go into teach yoga classes, I have to hook up the speakers, turn on the lights for find my space in the park. So many things may go differently than I could imagine. I show up with an openness to just allow whatever happens.

Leadership isn't about perfection—it's about presence, intention, and acting in alignment with your values. Even small choices—like offering help to someone new in the room or asking a thoughtful question—can make a big impact. Showing up intentionally also means honoring yourself:

- Listening to my body and pacing myself when needed
- Pausing when fatigue or overwhelm hit
- Accepting that I didn't have to do everything

How does it show up for you? How do you honor what you notice and adjust?

Advantages of Being Intentional

By focusing on intention, you create space for growth, learning, and connection. Showing up is not about impressing others—it's about respecting yourself, being present, and stepping into the moment fully. This brings me back to the core of Healthy & Fun Choices. Just as I intentionally bring focus, presence, and courage to a conference or a coaching session, we can intentionally bring these principles into everyday life—our movement, recovery, nutrition, and relationships.

When we show up as we are, we're not just surviving; we're actively building our legacy.

Chapter 21

Leading with Love

Living with intention means more than knowing what's healthy or fun—it's about weaving those choices into the very fabric of your daily life. This chapter explores how to bring Healthy & Fun Choices into different areas, from sleep and rest to minimizing screen time and EMF exposure. It's about creating spaces—whether inside or outside your home—that nurture your body, mind, and spirit. Imagine a backyard with a cozy patio, a deck for entertaining, hammocks for reading or napping, playful spaces for pets, and areas that invite movement and joy.

By intentionally designing your routines and environments, you give yourself the freedom to live fully, feel rested, and enjoy life's little pleasures every day.

Creating Evening Routines and Sleep Sanctuary
Setting designated times for being offline and limiting screen time on electronic devices can have several health benefits. It allows for dedicated periods of rest and promotes a healthier balance between technology use and other activities.

Taking breaks from electronic devices can help reduce stress, improve mental clarity, and enhance overall well-being. It allows for time to engage in other activities such as hobbies, exercise, or spending quality time with loved ones. The blue light emitted by electronic devices, including cell phones and computers, can interfere with the body's natural sleep-wake cycle.

Establishing a device-free period before bedtime promotes better sleep quality by reducing exposure to stimulating light and giving the mind a chance to unwind. While the debate on the health effects of EMFs continues, some studies suggest that prolonged exposure to high levels of electromagnetic radiation may have potential risks. By putting away cell phones and turning off Wi-Fi at night, you can reduce exposure to EMFs and create a more conducive sleep environment.

Setting a timer or using apps that track screen time can help increase awareness of how much time is spent on electronic devices. This promotes mindful technology use and can help prevent excessive usage that may interfere with daily routines, productivity, and personal relationships.

It's important to note that the link between EMF exposure and DNA damage is still a topic of ongoing scientific research and debate. While it's advisable to limit exposure to electromagnetic radiation, further studies are needed to establish conclusive evidence regarding its long-term effects on human health.
In summary, incorporating device-free periods, reducing screen time, and being mindful of technology use can contribute to a healthier lifestyle, better sleep, and a more balanced approach to integrating technology into daily routines.

Creating Your Backyard, Your Way
So many times we look at places we can go hiking or parks we can hang out in, when really we could create a park or fun space in our own backyard! How can you create a backyard that you want to spend more time in?

We have a big concrete patio and so this summer prior to my daughters high school graduation, I created a make-shift fence from used pallets and hung a string of lights up high to create a magical dance floor for country line dancing. It provided a lot of fun and entertainment beyond the party. In the summer it provided a nice spot for friends to come over and have dinner and now in the fall it provides a little extra light in the evening.

Exercising Ideas at Home
My cousin installed imitation grass with a big springboard underneath so his kids could roll around and jump in the backyard. He also installed climbing bars and big swings. Giving kids ways to climb, play, explore, and try new activities is such a great idea! His kids, now in high school and college, are creative and strong. They excel in sports and school.

Some people like to turn their garage or their basement into a work out area. They may put down rubber click-together flooring or add a weight bench, cycling system or treadmill. I remember when I was a kid, we had a basement with a workout machine, weights we could lift, and a pull-up bar at the door. It was a great way to connect with my parents and brothers as we could talk while exercising—maybe even doing sit-up challenges together. What are some ways you could integrate fitness into your home? Can you create a space to lift weights or have a pull-up bar? Are you able to put in a climbing wall or monkey bars?

Sacred Spaces
Last year I found an electric fireplace that looks real. I put it in my office and got an area rug to put in front of it. A couple of bean bag chairs and my yoga mat creates a nice space for meditation, relaxation and even yoga. My office desk is off to the side and having the sacred space actually allows my office work to feel more relaxed and purposeful. Since it is electric I can also roll it into my bedroom and enjoy the heat as I slow down in the evenings.

Each season I try to adjust my home design to colors and styles that complement the season. Additionally I like to rearrange my garage so that the products we use the most are closest for access. When it is ski season, the shelves nearest the garage door hold our boots, bags and our skis nearby. When it is summer, the shelves hold our life jackets, inflatable kayaks and camping gear.

My bedroom is the same way, I move my clothes around depending on what season it is and what I want to look at. My bed covers change to warm and fuzzy in the winter and light and airy in the summer. It all depends on where you live and how the weather changes. You may want to start considering how you can intentionally adjust your home to make it support your healthy and fun choices.

My son is an excellent example of wanting to be mindful about the foods that he is taking in. With his desire to be fit and healthy, he has helped us get rid of sugary and starchy foods that don't support whole health.

Our snack drawer is now full of energy bars, popcorn, and dried fruit or nuts. We have a smoothie-making station with protein powder, peanut butter, and bananas near each other so it is easy to make, put away the products and clean the mixer for the next time. We have a rule to try to clean right away afterwards because it is easier and takes less time.

Our refrigerator at times has been meal prepped and we do our best to choose colorful veggies, proteins and fish that support healthy growing bodies. What ways can you create your kitchen for living and eating with intention? How can you proactively create a good space to eat and feel supported?

Having a bathroom that is clean and products available is less stressful when you are in a hurry. We are very visual people, so we tend to use clear boxes or holders for all that we need right at our finger tips. Our drawers hold back-up products or items that we don't have to have right there. When we have too many products, we feel overwhelmed so we reduce that situation. What can you do in the bathroom to make it feel good? How can you make it easier for people to change the toilet paper when it runs out? It's the little things that count! A couple weeks ago I was in a hotel that had two toilet paper rolls, one was going forward and one backwards. You decide which is which, but I thought that was really clever. No one gets upset over their different choices.

Work of the Home
I love this concept that the Montessori pedagogy introduced: instead of chores it is called work of the home. Everyone participates and it is a shared experience. It isn't a chore, it is just a way of living. Other cultures also integrate in cleaning as part of daily living. Like sweeping the floors after a meal. Cleaning the toilet after using it. The list goes on. One of my goals this year is cleaning up after I use it and putting away dishes prior to going to bed. It is helping me come into the kitchen with more ease and joy. My question to you: Is the glass half empty or half full? What if it really doesn't matter because it is just a glass with water in it and the longer you hold it out there, the heavier it gets. Is it your responsibility or someone else to do the chores?

I believe we waste more time than we should trying to figure out chores than just doing them. What small tasks or charts or conversations can you have to just begin. How can you adjust your time so that the chores get done proactively rather than reacting about them not being done? Take note of your changes and how it may improve your life.

Recycling, reusing, and re-purposing aren't just good for the planet—they're ways to bring mindfulness and creativity into everyday life. When we reuse items, we extend their life and reduce waste. When we recycle, we transform materials into new products, conserving resources and energy. And when we repurpose, we give objects a second life in ways that can be functional, beautiful, or even playful—like turning an old ladder into a bookshelf or mason jars into planters. Each choice, no matter how small, contributes to a healthier environment, encourages intentional living, and reminds us that sustainability can be practical, rewarding, and fun.

Every small adjustment we make—whether it's choosing to recycle, creating a cozy backyard retreat, minimizing screen time, or adding spaces that bring joy—ripples outward.

These intentional choices don't just improve our own homes; they foster healthier communities and a more sustainable world. Each action, no matter how small, contributes to a collective shift toward well-being, connection, and care. *When we take these steps together, we create a world that is not only healthier but also more joyful.*

Use this space to draw out ideas on creating spaces that honor who you are and what you want...

Chapter 22

Pets as Companions

Do you have pets? If so, you know the joy, laughter, and love they bring. If not, even thinking about caring for a pet or helping with someone else's pet can add small but meaningful moments of connection and care. Pets aren't just animals—they are companions, teachers, and sources of comfort. They encourage us to slow down, to play, and to nurture, often teaching lessons we didn't realize we needed to learn.

My dog offers me love, respect, and companionship every day. She's my partner on walks, leading me to discover new trails and places to explore. She stays by my side during meals (hoping for leftovers) and even helps herd our ducks in the yard. Pets like her remind us to be present and to appreciate the simple joys of life.

Benefits of Different Types of Pets
Pets can also be incredible teachers. Caring for a pet: feeding the dog, changing the cat litter, or playing with a bunny helps kids learn responsibility, empathy, and the value of routines. Pets encourage us to take breaks from our busy lives, simply because they need attention. Sometimes we are reminded to slow down, sit on the floor, or enjoy a quiet cuddle. If you don't have a pet, volunteering or helping a friend care is fun!

Pets also teach us about loss and resilience. Their lifespans are shorter than ours, and the sadness that comes with losing a pet can be profound. When our dog broke his leg in a tough accident, through tears, care, and patience, our family bonded more closely with our pet, and my daughter learned compassion and responsibility. Experiences like these shaped her path—she later pursued farm studies and a career caring for animals.

Even smaller pets can make a big impact. For years, we had a fish tank. The gentle bubbling created a soothing background in our home, while feeding and naming the fish became a source of entertainment and storytelling. Fish remind us to observe, reflect, and create fun, imaginative connections even with creatures that don't cuddle or walk beside us.

Dogs, cats, ferrets, or talking birds—can also expand our social circles. I've met countless people at dog parks and through creating dog camps for kids. Pets can be bridges to community, conversation, and new friendships.

Dogs: True companions. Loyal, funny, protective, and loving. Dogs encourage movement, outdoor exploration, and social connections.

Cats: Entertaining and independent, with big personalities. They love attention on their own terms and bring joy through play and cuddles.

Bunnies: Soft, curious, and gentle. Caring for a bunny encourages mindfulness, patience, and nurturing skills.

Reptiles: Fascinating and low-maintenance. Reptiles provide entertainment, teach observation, and responds to gentle handling.

Birds: Intelligent, sometimes talkative, and full of personality. Birds can entertain, mimic sounds, and offer companionship with a lighter footprint.

Fish: Calm and visually soothing. Watching fish or listening to tank bubbles reduces stress, creates background relaxation, and sparks creativity in storytelling or home décor.

Ferrets: Energetic, personable, and mischievous. Ferrets bring laughter, encourage playful interaction, and make great interactive companions.

Pets and Play
Play is central to both human and animal well-being. Interacting with pets encourages movement, mental stimulation, and joy. Whether it's tossing a ball for a dog, dangling a feather for a cat, or watching a ferret explore a maze, these moments are not just fun—they are restorative. Play with pets is also a reminder to embrace spontaneity, curiosity, and joy in everyday life.

Pets and Life Lessons
Pets teach us lessons about compassion, responsibility, and resilience. Caring for them requires routines and consistency, helping children and adults alike develop structure in their lives. They teach empathy by showing us how to respond to needs, discomfort, and joy. Pets also remind us to celebrate small wins—a successful litter cleanup, a bunny hopping freely, or a dog mastering a new trick.

Pets are more than companions; they are teachers, friends, and playful co-creators in our lives. They bring joy, comfort, and love, and encourage us to move, rest, and engage with the world around us. By welcoming pets into our homes or supporting animals in our communities, we create opportunities for growth, connection, and shared happiness.

Integrating Pets into a Healthy & Fun Lifestyle

Whether it's a dog nudging you to go for a walk, a cat curling on your lap, or a fish tank bubbling in the background, pets remind us to slow down, enjoy the moment, and celebrate the joy of simple, loving presence.

Create Playful Spaces at Home: Design areas where pets can explore safely. A cozy corner with toys for cats or ferrets, a sandbox for rabbits, or a small pond for fish can encourage natural behaviors and reduce stress. Outdoor spaces with patios, decks, or hammocks can be shared for playtime and relaxation.

Schedule Daily Movement: Pets, especially dogs, encourage regular walks and outdoor activity. Even short walks or interactive indoor play sessions can boost your fitness, mood, and connection with your pet.

Engage in Interactive Play: Use games that stimulate both body and mind. Feather wands for cats, agility courses for dogs, or puzzle feeders for rabbits and birds help keep pets mentally sharp and entertained.

Include Kids in Care Routines: Feeding, grooming, litter cleaning, and general care teach responsibility, empathy, and the value of nurturing. Rotate responsibilities to create shared ownership of pet well-being.

Prioritize Recovery and Rest: Pets often model rest and mindfulness. Encourage them to have cozy spots for naps, and use that as a cue for your own downtime or meditation practice.

Celebrate Milestones and Achievements: Training a pet, teaching new tricks, or achieving consistent care routines can be rewarding for both humans and animals. Celebrate progress, not just outcomes.

Use Pets as a Social Bridge: Walking dogs, attending pet-friendly events, or participating in community volunteer opportunities can help you meet new people and build lasting connections.

Mindful Observation and Connection: Spend a few minutes each day observing your pet—watching fish swim, noticing a bird's behaviors, or simply sitting with your dog or cat. These moments cultivate mindfulness, reduce stress, and deepen bond.

Support Pet Health for Mutual Well-Being: Routine veterinary visits, proper nutrition, and vaccinations help ensure your pets live long, healthy lives—so your time together remains joyful and fulfilling.

Remember Fun and Joy Are Part of Health
Pets remind us that healthy living doesn't have to be serious. Laughter, play, and affection are essential for emotional and physical well-being—for both you and your animal companions.

Integrating pets into your life isn't just about care—it's about creating a lifestyle that nurtures love, movement, play, and connection. When we intentionally make space for pets in our homes, routines, and hearts, we bring more joy, mindfulness, and balance into our daily lives.

Check out the activity workbook called Healthy Pets. Healthy Families. I created it when I was teaching Pet Camps at FMES and Alpenrose Dairy for 4H. We had wonderful dog camps and pet camps with fun activities, lessons, and I think children that came dressed up as dogs! It is a wonderful activity book for kids that can be found in Amazon or your local retail location. It is a conversation starter and fun to do together with your kids, give as a gift or even use in a preschool or school setting.

What could you create in your home or lifestyle so your pets are a nurturing part of your life?

You can also use this space to draw a picture of your pet or a pet that you would love to have!

Chapter 23

Nurture Nature

Nature is more than a backdrop—it's a teacher, a healer, and a mirror for our own growth. Every hike through the woods, paddle across a lake, or quiet moment under the night sky offers lessons about resilience, patience, and presence. By intentionally connecting with the natural world, we uncover Brilliant You—a self fully integrated with life's rhythms and wonders.

Seasonal Adventures and Lessons

Spring: Hiking to Waterfalls
Spring is a season of renewal. One memorable morning, I hiked to a hidden waterfall as the forest floor bloomed with tender green shoots. The air was crisp, carrying the scent of damp earth and new growth. Standing at the waterfall's edge, I watched the water carve its path over rocks with steady persistence. Nature reminded me that growth takes time, and that even powerful transformations can flow gently and consistently. The vibrant energy of spring encouraged me to start new projects and fresh possibilities, just as the forest embraces new life.

Summer: Stargazing from a Hammock
Summer evenings invite us to slow down and look up. I remember lying in a hammock under a wide, star-studded sky, the warm air brushing my skin, and feeling the gentle hum of cicadas. Watching falling stars streak across the darkness reminded me of possibility and wonder—the universe vast and full of potential. Summer, with its long days and abundant warmth, teaches joy, exploration, and the value of quiet reflection amid busyness.

Autumn: Observing Leaves Change

Autumn brings vibrant colors and a lesson in letting go. Hiking through the woods during this season, I watched leaves turn brilliant reds, golds, and oranges before falling to the forest floor. Like the mangroves whose yellowing leaves nourish younger ones, these fallen leaves provide warmth and sustenance to the earth for the next season. Autumn reminds us that release is necessary for growth and that every ending contains the seed of a new beginning. Sometimes I will collect leaves and bring them indoors, we will dry them and then sandwich them between contact paper to make lovely window designs or place mats.

Winter: Skiing and Mountain Views

Winter offers clarity and perspective. Skiing along mountain tops, feeling the cold wind, and seeing snow-blanketed landscapes stretching for miles gives a sense of expansiveness and resilience. The mountains remind us to rise to challenges, gain perspective, and embrace the stillness that allows reflection and preparation for new growth. Winter encourages patience, mindfulness, and the wisdom that rests before renewal.

Learning from nature begins with the simple act of slowing down and noticing. When you step outside with curiosity—whether you're standing at the water's edge, sitting under a tree, or walking along a trail—you start to see how the natural world responds to challenge, change, and time. Nature becomes a teacher not through explanation, but through example. The Healthy & Fun Choices Way invites you to treat these quiet moments outside as opportunities to understand yourself better, reconnect with your breath, and discover the wisdom that already surrounds you.

Spend time near water and observe how it moves. Notice how a river flows around the rocks in its way instead of fighting them, or how the tide rises and falls in its own rhythm. Even the plants at the shoreline offer lessons—roots gripping deep into the earth while still allowing movement with the waves. You begin to see resilience in the way water adapts, patience in its steady persistence, and calm in the natural ebb and flow. These moments remind us that we, too, can keep moving forward even when the path isn't straight.

Look up and pay attention to the sky—how clouds reshape themselves, how the wind shifts directions, or how the night sky expands far beyond what we can comprehend. Air and sky teach presence, flexibility, and perspective. A single breeze can reset your body; a passing cloud can remind you that change never stays still; a moment under the stars can shrink your worries in the best way. Nature invites you to be here, right now, without needing to fix or analyze anything.

As you walk, notice the ground beneath you. Soil, sand, and forest floors all hold stories of growth, decay, and renewal. Every tree stands because the earth nourished its roots; every leaf falls because the season asked it to. Watching leaves change color, drop, and return again the following year offers one of nature's most powerful lessons: letting go is not losing—it's making space for what's next. These cycles teach us that growth often comes after release, and that rest is just as important as effort.

Even mountains and birds share their wisdom if you pause long enough to observe them. Mountains teach endurance—not through rushing to the summit, but through steady steps and patience with the climb. Birds remind us that everyone moves differently: some soar effortlessly, some flap with determination, and some hover joyfully in place. There is no one correct way to navigate the world, just your pace and current season of life.

When you allow nature to be your guide, you start to see lessons in everything: resilience, flexibility, grounding, courage, release, renewal. These lessons don't require any special equipment or training. They simply ask you to step outside, breathe, observe, and let the world teach you in its patient, effortless way.

As you've moved through this book, you've been gathering new ways of seeing yourself and the world around you. By now, you may be noticing that nature is not just something outside of you — it is something you are connected to, shaped by, and restored through. Whether it's the way a river keeps moving forward, the way a tree finds balance in the wind, or the way the seasons rise and fall, the natural world reminds us that healing and growth are not tasks to accomplish but rhythms to join.

Nature doesn't ask you to be perfect; it simply invites you to be present, observant, and willing to learn from what it generously offers. -Kirsten Klug

When you choose to spend even a few mindful moments outdoors, you begin to feel how deeply nature supports your becoming. A walk on a familiar trail reveals new details when you pay attention. Sitting by water helps you reconnect with the ease of flow and breath. A night sky expands your perspective and invites wonder. The changing seasons reflect your own cycles of growth, rest, release, and renewal. Birds remind you of lightness and courage; the earth beneath your feet grounds you in your own strength. These experiences don't have to be grand or dramatic — they work quietly, in the background, shaping you in subtle, powerful ways.

As you lean more fully into these connections, you begin to recognize that you are also part of this living, breathing landscape. You have roots, wings, tides, and seasons. You have moments when you rise, moments when you rest, and moments when you transform. The brilliance within you is not separate from the world you step into — it is woven into the same wisdom that guides rivers, mountains, leaves, and stars. When you honor this connection, you step into a more mindful, creative, joyful way of living — one that feels true not just in your habits, but in your heart.

This is the essence of the Healthy & Fun Choices Way: noticing, learning, and allowing yourself to belong deeply to both your inner world and the natural world around you. You are becoming someone who listens to the earth, who learns from movement and stillness, who honors their own cycles, and who trusts that growth continues in unexpected ways. Let nature keep teaching you — through each walk, each breath of fresh air, each change in light or season.

Just remember, when you need guidance, inspiration, or a gentle reminder of your own resilience, you can return to these pages, or explore more practices and nature-based reflections at HealthyFunChoices.com and anywhere you may find more.

***You are growing, becoming, and finding your way—
beautifully, naturally, and fully connected.***

Just like the nurse log that falls to the forest floor, we, too, can deepen our love for ourselves— becoming a source of warmth, nourishment, and perfect ground for new growth. The Healthy & Fun Choices Way gently returns us to recognizing our own beauty, resilience, and ever-unfolding growth.
  —Kirsten Klug

Chapter 24

The Healthy & Fun Choices Way is now... Brilliant YOU!

This book is about finding joy on purpose and living a little braver each day. The Healthy & Fun Choices Way is your path back home to yourself.

Bravery rarely looks like the grand, dramatic gestures we picture in our mind. More often, it looks like remembering who you are, even when your world feels loud or overwhelming. It looks like making small choices that help you show up with more presence, more intention, and more heart. It looks like trusting that you don't need to fix yourself before you start living. You begin exactly where you are — messy, beautiful, human — and you allow yourself to grow forward.

When we choose to live heart-centered, something shifts. Life stops feeling like a race to prove ourselves and begins to feel like a steady unfolding. You give yourself permission to show up without needing every answer or every detail sorted. You start noticing what supports you instead of what is wrong with you. And in that noticing, you soften. You breathe more. You judge less. You move through the world with the quiet confidence of someone who knows they belong.

Living braver isn't about eliminating fear; it's about creating space to hold both courage and fear in the same breath. When you show up to open up, even a little, life meets you halfway. Perhaps it's a conversation that finally feels honest. A first step toward something that once felt impossible.

A moment where you say yes to connection, even while your knees shake. You don't need to be fearless to be brave.

Fun is often dismissed as trivial, but it is one of the greatest tools for transformation. When you just add fun, your shoulders drop, your creativity awakens, and your energy begins to rise again. Fun lightens heavy moments and reminds you that joy is not something to earn, but something to allow. Laughter, playfulness, and curiosity all create room for growth. A little fun can shift everything—your mood, your day, and what is possible.

Caring for your body is another way of caring for your future self. Colorful foods invite energy back into your life, while the right kind of movement strengthens your ability to trust your body again. FUNctional fitness isn't about perfection, performance, or comparison—it's about movement that supports your whole life, not just the part others can see. It's about encouraging your muscles, joints, breath, and heart to work together so you can live with more vitality.

Joy deepens when you slow down long enough to enjoy the view around you. Sometimes this means pausing on a trail, noticing sunlight through trees, or catching a breath before rushing to the next thing. Other times it means savoring the sweetness in an ordinary moment — a warm drink, a heartfelt conversation, a quiet sunrise that arrives without asking for applause. Every day offers views worth noticing. Life becomes richer when you choose to see them.

Yoga, breath, rest, and restoration bring you back into your body and into your present moment of life. Rest is not a reward. Rest is a foundation. It is where recalibration happens, where clarity returns, and where your nervous system learns to trust safety again. When you honor rest, your mind expands, your spirit lifts, and your capacity for joy grows. There is strength in slowing down. There is courage in restoring. There is wisdom in listening inwardly for what you truly need.

All of this leads here—to the recognition that you are, and have always been, a brilliant you. Not a perfect you. Not an improved you. Simply the real, present, honest version of yourself, fully allowed to exist. When you stop trying to be what you think others expect, you reclaim your energy. When you stop apologizing for your imperfections, you discover your power. When you choose from a place of curiosity rather than self-judgment, your life begins to open.

You are not behind. You are not broken. You haven't missed your moment. You are a whole person learning how to trust your heart, one day at a time. That is brilliance. That is resilience. That is healing. That is growth.

The Healthy & Fun Choices Way is not a system to memorize or a checklist to complete. It's a practice of returning to yourself with compassion, courage, joy, and breath. It's a way of living that honors your body, your mind, your heart, and your relationships. It's a reminder that the choices you make—the small ones, the gentle ones, the consistent ones—shape the way you experience your life.

And the truth is: you are already doing this. You are already showing up. You are already learning, healing, trying, shifting, and choosing. You are already moving toward a life that feels more like you. You don't need to become someone new — you simply need to recognize the brilliance that has been here all along.

You are capable of beautiful things. You are worthy of your own love and attention. You are allowed to live a joyful, curious, brave life. And you are more than enough — exactly as you are, right now, in this moment.

Brilliant you.   **Always.**

A day lived through your Brilliant You doesn't require perfection. It simply asks for presence. It's the soft awareness that your choices matter, that you matter, and that your life is built moment by moment, breath by breath. When you begin to see yourself this way, even the smallest routines become invitations to return home to who you really are.

Imagine ending your evening by reviewing tomorrow with a gentle heart. You brush your teeth, drink a little water, gather the things that help you sleep—your red light therapy, your apnea machine, your favorite pillow. You plug in your phone, set your alarm, and let the room soften around you. As you settle into bed, you feel gratitude for this quiet moment. You close your eyes knowing that rest is a choice, and that rest is a tool. You wake with a soft smile, noticing the light filtering into your room, the stillness, the support of familiar objects. Morning begins not with a rush, but with awareness. You make breakfast, stretch while the coffee brews, watch your cat tracking birds through the window, laugh at the tiny playfulness of it all. These moments are not trivial—they are reminders that your day begins with intention.

Later, you step outside for a walk, leash in hand, your dog moving beside you with effortless trust. You follow your familiar path but stay open to whatever changes the day brings—a shift in the wind, a new route, a conversation with a neighbor. You notice colors, textures, sunlight through trees, the quiet rhythm of your own footsteps. When you pause for a crosswalk or look up at a towering fir, you give yourself permission to be present. You don't rush. You don't force. You simply walk as a person who knows their own pace. Time expands when you honor it this way.

At work—or on the mountain, or wherever your day leads— you arrive with a clear mind. You tidy the space around you, arrange your notes, glance at the reminders you've placed on your walls and decide which ones still support you and which ones you can lovingly let go. You greet your coworkers, call a client, or settle into the meeting ahead. There is a steadiness in you now, a sense of grounding that comes from choosing how you want to feel rather than reacting to everything around you. You focus on what matters most and allow yourself to move through the day with intention instead of urgency.

If you are parenting or caregiving, you begin by tending to yourself first. A glass of water. A few stretches. A moment to breathe before tending to those who rely on you. You know you bring your best self when you feel grounded, and you know on the hard days—because they happen—you can pause, breathe, and invite them to pause with you. Maybe the moment calls for stepping outside to listen to birds, or feeling the breeze, or simply letting tears fall. The gift of your Brilliant You is not that you avoid hard moments, but that you meet them honestly, gently, and without judgment.

There are days when your Brilliant You shows up not through tasks or routines, but through the simple act of creating. You sit at a table with a notebook, a sketchpad, a brush, or even a sticky note, and allow yourself to follow whatever wants to emerge. It might be a phrase, a doodle, a grocery list written more beautifully than necessary, or the beginning of an idea you didn't realize was waiting.

Creativity doesn't ask for permission or perfection—it just asks for presence. When you take a moment to draw, paint, write, sing, arrange flowers, photograph a shadow, or dance in the kitchen while making lunch, you invite joy to move through you. You become a witness to your own aliveness. The world gets quieter. Your breath slows. And instead of needing to "do" anything, you simply "be." These moments, however small, are where your truth finds space to glow again.

       This is your Brilliant You at play.

There are also days when your Brilliant You speaks in whispers, inviting you to rest. Not because you're weak or behind, but because your body and heart are wise. You might wake up with heavy limbs, a foggy mind, or emotion sitting closer to the surface than usual. Instead of fighting it, you pause. You breathe. You honor the pace your body is asking for.

Rest can look like curling up under a blanket, stretching gently on the living room floor, stepping outside to feel the sun or rain on your skin, or letting yourself savor the quiet between obligations. Recovery isn't a step backward—it's the place where integration happens. It's the moment the body repairs, the nervous system recalibrates, and the mind remembers it doesn't have to carry everything alone. When you give yourself permission to rest without guilt, you reconnect with your deeper strength. You awaken again, not because you pushed through, but because you listened inwardly.

Some days, your Brilliant You shows up in the company you keep. You walk into a café and are met with a warm smile from a barista who remembers your order. You send a message to a friend just because their name rose to the surface of your mind. You listen—really listen—to your partner, your child, your neighbor, or a coworker. And they soften in your presence.

Connection isn't measured by how many people you know—it's felt in the quality of the moments you share. When you let yourself be both honest and open, even for a breath, you create space for others to do the same. These experiences remind you that belonging is not something you chase; it's something you create by showing up with your whole heart.

Your Brilliant You shows up in countless ways—movement, stillness, creativity, connection, work, play, rest, and every choice in between. When you begin to see these moments not as tasks, but as opportunities to return to yourself, your days unfold with more ease, clarity, and possibility. **You start to recognize that the magic isn't in doing more—it's in being more present for what's already here.** Every day unfolds differently, yet the practice of The Healthy & Fun Choices Way remains the same.

Begin with awareness: What is here?

Continue with acceptance: Where am I?

Move with intention: How do I want to show up?

Respond with compassion: Who am I becoming?

Return with gratitude: When do I feel most like myself?

This is why the Healthy & Fun Choices Way matters. It brings you back to peace, joy, breath, and love. It invites you to show up fully—not in spite of your imperfections, but because of your humanity. It teaches you that your life is made of choices you can meet with kindness, one moment at a time.

You are the one who gets to shape your days.

You are the one who gets to decide
how you move through the world.

Every time you choose presence,
curiosity, and love—you live as the

Brilliant You you were meant to be.

*"When a heart-shaped leaf
drifts into
your path,
let it gently remind you
to pause,
return to brilliant you,
and breathe in…
and out."*

— Kirsten Klug

Chapter 25
Just Breathe

Quiet reflection is not a luxury—it's a return. Whenever you feel yourself rushing, comparing, doubting, or wondering if you're doing life "right," remember that there is no right way. There is only your way. And your way begins with a breath.

Just breathe.
Slowly.
Softly.

Fully.

    Breath is the bridge back to presence. It anchors you when life feels busy and settles you when your mind tries to race ahead. Before events, before coaching, before teaching, and even before opening this book, I've learned that showing up begins with breathing. One inhale to gather yourself.
                          One exhale to open.
    Find a comfortable position, relax your shoulders, and place your hands where they feel at home—maybe on your lap or your heart. Notice the rise and fall of your breath. Slow it down if you'd like. Let your shoulders drop a little more. Let your mind soften. Let your body feel held.

You are here.
        You are safe.
                You are enough.

Just breathe.

As you inhale, imagine drawing in clarity and calm. As you exhale, imagine releasing everything that's asking to be set down. Wiggle your toes to reconnect with your body. Gently shift your gaze to take in the space around you. Let yourself return with a little more compassion, a little more grace, and a little more awareness.

Your breath is always available to guide you back home. Whenever you forget who you are, or feel unsure of your next step, breathe. It will remind you of your brilliance. Practice here.

Closing Reflection

As you move through your days, remember that brilliance isn't about perfection—it's about presence. It's the quiet courage of showing up as you are, breathing fully, and meeting each moment with curiosity instead of fear. You don't have to rush toward the future or try to become who you once were. You get to be here, now, aware, alive, and connected to the rhythms that guide every living thing.

When catch the glimpse of a leaf drifting to the ground, when your dog races to greet you, when laughter fills the room, or when you pause at the top of a mountain before carving into a run, let those moments remind you of your own aliveness. These flashes of wonder reflect who you are becoming—growing, evolving, and shining in your own natural, unhurried way.

Just as seeds soften underground before they rise, and flowers turn toward the sun without questioning their path, you are continually becoming. You are creating the life you love, and learning to love the life you create.

One breath, one choice, one moment at a time—your Brilliant You is already here.

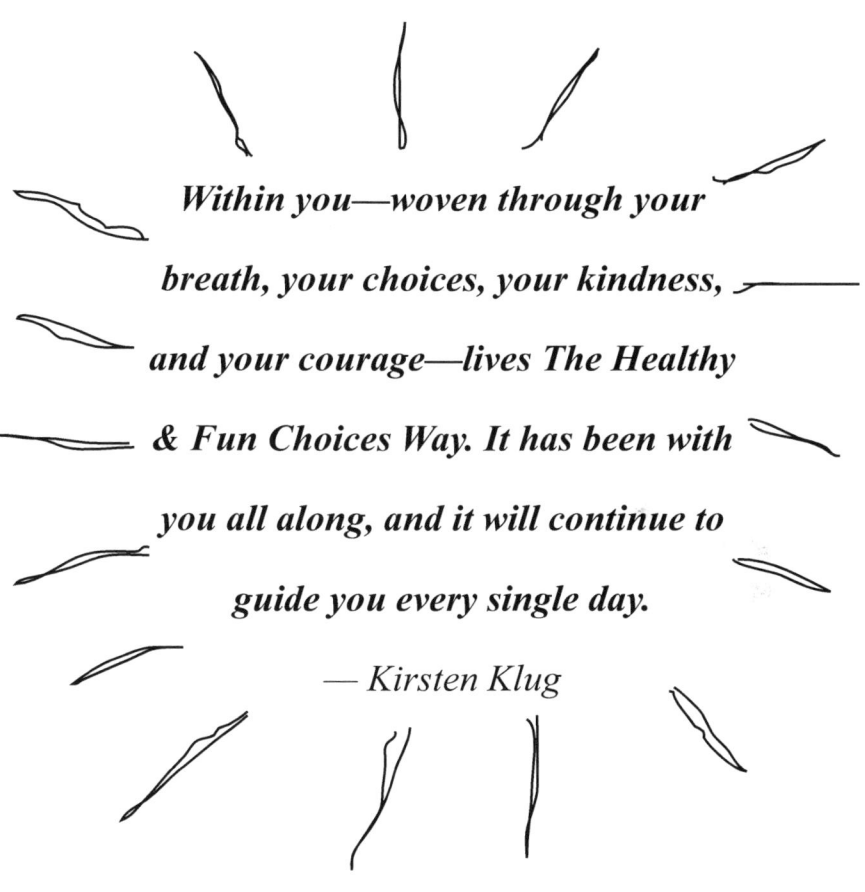

Within you—woven through your breath, your choices, your kindness, and your courage—lives The Healthy & Fun Choices Way. It has been with you all along, and it will continue to guide you every single day.

— Kirsten Klug

About the Author

Kirsten Klug is a mompreneur, educator, designer, and storyteller whose lived experiences with chronic pain, multiple surgeries, and aphasia have shaped her into a compassionate advocate for resilience, creativity, and whole-health living. Her ability to simplify complex ideas into uplifting, accessible tools has made her a trusted voice for people seeking more joy, intention, and courage in their everyday lives.

After developing aphasia following significant medical trauma, Kirsten became a vocal advocate for communication confidence and brain-friendly living. As an Aphasia Ambassador, she teaches others how to find their voice again—through writing, speaking, listening, creative expression, and learning how to live with yourself gently on the days when the words won't come. She knows firsthand the courage it takes to share ideas when typing requires retyping, when speaking requires patience, and when the world doesn't always understand. Her work helps others feel seen, supported, and empowered in their own communication journeys.

She is the founder of The Healthy & Fun Choices® Way, a framework that helps people reconnect with themselves through movement, mindfulness, nature, positive communication, and heart-centered choices. Kirsten also created the Healthy & Fun App, a supportive tool for bringing intentional living into daily rhythms. In the outdoor world, she developed Slope Stewards™, a mountain-safety and culture program centered on awareness, kindness, leadership, and fun in alpine environments.

Kirsten speaks and teaches nationally on wellness, creative living, communication confidence, and braver living. Through her workshops, coaching, community programs, and books, she helps people of all ages navigate life's challenges with more presence, compassion, and joy. As someone who has rebuilt her life through brain changes, surgeries, trauma, healing, movement, love, and humor, she models what it means to keep showing up with grace.

She lives in Oregon, where she continues to write, coach, design, teach yoga, and explore the outdoors with her family—living proof that hope, strength, and joy can grow through every season of life.

Connect with Kirsten:
- Websites: HealthyFunChoices.com
- KirstenKlug.com
- Facebook: facebook.com/KirstenEKlug
- IG: instagram.com/KirstenInspires

Resources & Connections

Thank you for joining me on this journey. If you'd like to continue exploring The Healthy & Fun Choices Way, here are places and programs that support whole-health living books and communicating with confidence, and joyful, braver living. Books available on Amazon.com and HealthyFunChoices.com

Healthy & Fun Yoga & Mindset Classes with Kirsten
Join Kirsten for yoga, chair yoga, mindful movement, and breath-centered classes designed for people of all abilities.
- Mon & Wed nights 7-8pm at the Sunnyside Grange
- LoveYourBrain.org classes on Zoom
- Invite Kirsten to do a workshop or keynote

Aphasia Community Support Group
A supportive space for individuals and caregivers. 2nd Wed 2:15–3:00 pm at the Milwaukie Community Center

LoveYourBrain Foundation
A powerful community offering yoga, mindfulness, and support for individuals and families affected by brain injury.
www.LoveYourBrain.com

National Aphasia Association (NAA)
Resources, education, and support for people living with aphasia and their families. Learn more at Aphasia.org

Slope Stewards™
A mountain-safety and culture program designed to build awareness, leadership, and fun on the slopes.SlopeStewards.com

Made in the USA
Coppell, TX
08 December 2025

64830981R00139